𝔊𝔬𝔩𝔲𝔪𝔟𝔦𝔞 𝔘𝔫𝔦𝔟𝔢𝔯𝔰𝔦𝔱𝔶 𝔏𝔢𝔠𝔱𝔲𝔯𝔢𝔰

# CONSTITUTIONAL GOVERNMENT IN THE UNITED STATES

## GEORGE BLUMENTHAL FOUNDATION

1907

COLUMBIA UNIVERSITY PRESS
SALES AGENTS

NEW YORK
LEMCKE & BUECHNER
30–32 EAST 20TH STREET

LONDON
HUMPHREY MILFORD
AMEN CORNER, E.C.

SHANGHAI
EDWARD EVANS & SONS, LTD.
30 NORTH SZECHUEN ROAD

COLUMBIA UNIVERSITY LECTURES

# CONSTITUTIONAL GOVERNMENT IN THE UNITED STATES

BY

## WOODROW WILSON, Ph.D., LL.D.
PRESIDENT OF PRINCETON UNIVERSITY

New York

COLUMBIA UNIVERSITY PRESS

1921
3/26

Norwood Press
J. S. Cushing Co. — Berwick & Smith Co.
Norwood, Mass., U.S.A.

# PREFATORY NOTE

THESE lectures are not intended as a systematic discussion of the character and operation of the government of the United States. They are intended merely to present it in some of its more salient features from a fresh point of view and in the light of a fresh analysis of the character and operation of constitutional government. It is hoped that they will be thought, for this reason, to be serviceable in the clarification of our views as to policy and practice.

WOODROW WILSON.

PRINCETON, NEW JERSEY,
March 24, 1908.

v

# CONTENTS

# CONSTITUTIONAL GOVERNMENT
# IN THE UNITED STATES

## I

### WHAT IS CONSTITUTIONAL GOVERNMENT?

26002

MY object in the following lectures is to examine the
government of the United States as a constitutional system
as simply and directly as possible, with an eye to practice,
not to theory.

And yet at the very outset it is necessary to pause upon
a theory. The government of the United States cannot
be intelligently discussed as a constitutional system until
we clearly determine what we mean by a "constitutional"
government; and the answer to that question is in effect
a theory of politics.

By a constitutional government we, of course, do not
mean merely a government conducted according to the
provisions of a definite constitution; for every modern
government with which our thoughts deal at all has a
definite constitution, written or unwritten, and we should
not dream of speaking of all modern governments as
"constitutional." Not even when their constitutions are
written with the utmost definiteness of formulation. The
constitution of England, the most famous of constitutional
governments and in a sense the mother of them all, is not

written, and the constitution of Russia might be without changing the essential character of the Czar's power. A constitutional government is one whose powers have been adapted to the interests of its people and to the maintenance of individual liberty. That, in brief, is the conception we constantly make use of, but seldom analyze, when we speak of constitutional governments.

Roughly speaking, constitutional government may be said to have had its rise at Runnymede, when the barons of England exacted Magna Carta of John; and that famous transaction we may take as the dramatic embodiment alike of the theory and of the practice we seek. The barons met John at Runnymede, a body of armed men in counsel, for a parley which, should it not end as they wished it to end, was to be but a prelude to rebellion. They were not demanding new laws or better, but a righteous and consistent administration of laws they regarded as already established, their immemorial birthright as Englishmen. They had found John whimsical, arbitrary, untrustworthy, never to be counted on to follow any fixed precedent or limit himself by any common understanding, a lying master who respected no man's rights and thought only of having his own will; and they came to have a final reckoning with him. And so they thrust Magna Carta under his hand to be signed, — a document of definition, which spoke of rights which had been disregarded and which must henceforth be respected, of practices until now indulged in which must be given over and remedied altogether, of ancient methods too long abandoned to which the king must return; and their proposal was this: 'Give us your solemn promise as monarch that this document shall be your guide and rule in all your dealings with us, attest that promise by your sign manual attached in solemn form, admit certain of our number a committee to observe the keeping of the covenant, and we are your subjects in all peaceful form and obedience; — refuse, and we are your enemies, absolved of our allegiance and free to choose a king who will rule us as he should.' Swords made uneasy stir in their scabbards, and John had no choice but to sign. These were the only terms upon which government could be conducted among Englishmen.

That was the beginning of constitutional government, and shows the nature of that government in its simplest form. There at Runnymede a people came to an understanding with its governors, and established once for all that ideal of government which we now call "constitutional," — the ideal of a government conducted upon the basis of a definite understanding, if need be of a formal pact, between those who are to submit to it and those who are to conduct it, with a view to making government an instrument of the general welfare rather than an arbitrary, self-willed master, doing what it pleases, — and particularly for the purpose of safeguarding individual liberty.

The immortal service of Magna Carta was its formulation of the liberties of the individual in their adjustment to the law. The day of Magna Carta was not a day in which men spoke of political liberty or acted upon set programs of political reform; but the history of constitutional government in the modern world is the history of political liberty, the history of all that men have striven for in the reform of government, and one has the right to expect to get out of it at least a workable conception of what liberty is. Certainly the documents of English history and the utterances of the greater public men on both sides of the water supply abundant material for the definition. "If any one ask me what a free government is, I reply, it is what the people think so," said Burke, going to the heart of the matter. The Declaration of Independence speaks to the same effect. We think of it as a highly theoretical document, but except for its assertion that all men are equal it is not. It is intensely practical, even upon the question of liberty. It names as among the "inalienable rights" of man the right to life, liberty, and the pursuit of happiness, as does the Virginia constitution and many another document of the time; but it expressly leaves to each generation of men the determination of what they will do with their lives, what they will prefer as the form and object of their liberty, in what they will seek their happiness. Its chief justification of the right of the colonists to break with the mother country is the assertion that men have always the right to determine for themselves by their own preferences and their own circumstances whether the government they live under is based upon such principles or administered according to such forms as are likely to effect their safety and happiness. In brief, political liberty is the right of those who are governed to adjust government to their own needs and interests.

That is the philosophy of constitutional government. Every generation, as Burke said, sets before itself some favorite object which it pursues as the very substance of its liberty and happiness. The ideals of liberty cannot be fixed from generation to generation; only its conception can be, the large image of what it is. Liberty fixed in unalterable law would be no liberty at all. Government is a part of life, and, with life, it must change, alike in its objects and in its practices; only this principle must remain unaltered, — this principle of liberty, that there must be the freest right and opportunity of adjustment. Political liberty consists in the best practicable adjustment between the power of the government and the privilege of the individual; and the freedom to alter the adjustment is as important as the adjustment itself for the ease and progress of affairs and the contentment of the citizen.

There are many analogies by which it is possible to illustrate the idea, if it needs illustration. We say of a boat skimming the water with light foot, 'How free she runs,' when we mean, how perfectly she is adjusted to the force of the wind, how perfectly she obeys the great breath out of the heavens that fills her sails. Throw her head up into the wind and see how she will halt and stagger, how every sheet will shiver and her whole frame be shaken, how instantly she is "in irons," in the expressive phrase of the sea. She is free only when you have let her fall off again and get once more her nice adjustment to the forces she must obey and cannot defy. We speak of the 'free' movement of the piston-rod in the perfectly made engine, and know of course that its freedom is proportioned to its perfect adjustment. The least lack of adjustment will heat it with friction and hold it stiff and unmanageable. There is nothing free in the sense of being unrestrained in a world of innumerable forces, and each force moves at its best when best adjusted to the forces about it. Spiritual things are not wholly comparable with material things, and political liberty is a thing of the spirits of men; but we speak of friction in things that affect our spirits, and do not feel that it is altogether a figure of speech. It is not forcing analogies, therefore, to say that that is the freest government in which there is the least friction, — the least friction between the power of the government and the privilege of the individual. The adjustment may vary from generation to generation, but the principle never can. A constitutional government, being an instrumentality for the maintenance of liberty, is an instrumentality for the maintenance of a right adjustment, and must have a machinery of constant adaptation.

English writers have not often enough noticed that in the very generation which saw Magna Carta formulated and signed in England, a similar transaction was witnessed in Hungary. Magna Carta was signed in 1215; seven years later, in 1222, the Magyar nobles of Hungary exacted of their king a document which ran upon singularly similar lines, a "Golden Bull," to which those who struggled for privilege in Hungary always looked back as Englishmen looked back to Magna Carta. But two remarkable differences existed between Magna Carta and the Golden Bull which it is worth while to dwell upon for a moment, because of their significance with regard to the question we are discussing, — the nature of constitutional government. For all she made a similar beginning, Hungary did not obtain constitutional government, and England did. Undoubtedly the chief reason was that the nobles of Hungary contended for the privileges of a class, while the barons of England contended for the privileges of a nation, and that the Englishmen were not seeking to set up any new law or privilege, but to recover and reëstablish what they already had and feared they should lose. Another and hardly less significant reason was that the Englishmen provided machinery for the maintenance of the agreement, and the Magyars did not.

Of course the parliament of England runs back in its origins beyond 1215; but the parliament which Simon of Montfort set up in 1265 and Edward confirmed in 1295 was the first that definitely received and accepted the trust of preserving the liberties, the free choices, of England against the wilful preferences of her kings, upon the basis laid in Magna Carta; and until that parliament was set up, with its burgesses and knights of the shire, the barons had attempted, as again and again they forced upon their kings a renewal of the great charter, to provide against its infringement by the watchfulness of representatives delegated from their own ranks to see that faith was kept. They had the practical instinct to see that promises upon paper are only promises upon paper, unless the party that demands privilege is as alert and as ready for action as the party that exercises power. The Magyar nobles provided no such machinery of maintenance and adjustment, and lost what they had gained. No doubt free parliaments are as important as definite charters.

And yet the other difference is the deeper and, in a sense, the more essential. The barons at Runnymede were not speaking for themselves as a class, but for Englishmen of every rank and privilege, and they were claiming nothing novel or of their own peculiar preference and invention, but rights which they conceived to be as old as Edward the Confessor. They were speaking, not out of theory, but out of practice and experience, for the maintenance of privileges which they conceived themselves time out of mind to have possessed. They were insisting that government should be adjusted to their actual lives, accommodated to their actual experience. And so Magna Carta speaks of no new rights. It grants nothing. It merely safeguards. It provides methods and reforms abuses. It does not say what men shall have by way of freedom and privilege; it speaks only of what restraints the king's government shall observe in seeking to abridge such freedom and privilege as Englishmen already of right enjoy. Let the famous 29th clause serve as an example. It says nothing of the grant to any man of life, liberty, or property: it takes it for granted that every man has the right to these, as our own Declaration of Independence does, and enacts simply that "no man shall be deprived of life, liberty, or property, save by the judgment of his peers and the law of the land." It is seeking to regulate the exercise of power, to adjust its operation, as safely and conveniently as may be, to that general interest which is the sum of the interest of every man; that he may be dealt with, not as the king arbitrarily pleases, but as his own peers, men of his own kind and interest, deem just, and as laws which deal equally with all men impartially direct.

Look into any constitutional document of the English-speaking race and you shall find the same spirit, the same way of action: its aim is always an arrangement, as if of business: no abstract setting forth of liberties, no pretense of grants of privilege or political rights, but always a formulation of limits and of methods, a regulation of the way governments shall act and individuals be dealt with. Take the first eight amendments to the Constitution of the United States as an example, and see in them the charter of liberties which the States insisted upon having added to the Constitution at the outset. The whole spirit and manner of the thing is exhibited in their businesslike phrases. "The right of the people to be secure in their persons, houses, papers, and effects, against unreasonable searches and seizures shall not be violated, and no warrants shall be issued but upon probable cause, supported by oath or affirmation, and particularly describing the places to be searched, and the persons or things to be seized," is the quiet language of the Fourth Amendment, denying to the government only unreasonable powers arbitrarily exercised. The words of the Fifth Article are equally business-like and sensible: "No person shall be held to answer for a capital, or otherwise infamous crime, unless on the presentment or indictment of a grand jury, except in cases arising in the land or naval forces, or in the militia, when in actual service in time of war or public danger; nor shall any person be subject for the same offense to be twice put in jeopardy of life or limb; nor shall be compelled in any criminal case to be a witness against himself; nor be deprived of life, liberty, or property, without due process of law; nor shall private property be taken for public use, without just compensation." Every clause bears the same practical character. Such provisions make of the Constitution an agreement as feasible and as acceptable as Magna Carta. It is a body of distinct stipulations as to where the lines of privilege shall run, where individual rights shall begin and governmental rights stop, in the more critical dealings between rulers and citizens.

And the whole of constitutional history is similarly concerned with definition, with method, with machinery, as if principles were taken for granted and no one doubted that men should be free, their interests righteously adjusted to the powers of government, securely safeguarded against governments' possible encroachments. The question of machinery, of ways and means, is manifestly of capital importance in a constitutional system. Such a system is based upon a definite understanding between governors and governed. No constitutional government has been without explicit written statements of the terms of the understanding such as is contained in Magna Carta. But it is important that these terms should be definite and unmistakable, not merely in order that disputes concerning its meaning and content may be avoided, but also in order that it may be clear what steps should be taken to carry it out; and the means provided for maintaining it in practice are hardly less indispensable than its own definitions. That is the reason why English constitutional history has centred about the development of parliament.

Not until after the Revolution of 1688 was parliament looked upon as modern Englishmen look upon it, as chiefly interesting because of the laws it could make. Not until the eighteenth century had passed its middle term did it come to be what it is now, the maker and unmaker of ministries, the maker and unmaker of governments. For at least four of the six hundred years during which it has been an instrument of constitutional government it was looked upon merely as the "grand assize," the great session, of the nation, whose function was criticism and restraint, which came together to see that the terms upon which English life was understood to rest were being scrupulously respected by the king and his advisers. The thought grew vague enough at times; the nation once and again lost consciousness of what its parliament meant; the parliament itself sometimes forgot for generations together what its trust and duty was; but every critical turn in affairs brought the whole impulse and conception sharply to light again, and the great tradition was never lost.

We speak now always of 'legislatures,' of 'law-*making*'

assemblies, are very impatient of prolonged debates, and sneer at parliamentary bodies which cannot get their 'business' done. We join with laughing zest in Mr. Carlyle's bitter gibe at "talking shops," at parliaments which spend their days in endless discussion rather than in diligent prosecution of what they came together to 'do.' And yet to hold such an attitude toward representative assemblies is utterly to forget their history and their first and capital purpose. They were meant to be talking shops. The name "parliament" is no accidental indication of their function. They were meant to be grand parleys with those who were conducting the country's business: parleys concerning laws, concerning administrative acts, concerning policies and plans at home and abroad, in order that nothing which contravened the common understanding should be let pass without comment or stricture, in order that measures should be insisted on which the nation needed, and measures resisted which the nation did not need or might take harm from. Their purpose was watchful criticism, talk that should bring to light the whole intention of the government and apprise those who conducted it of the real feeling and desire of the nation; and how well they performed that function many an uneasy monarch has testified, alike by word and act.

It was as far as possible from the original purpose of representative assemblies that they should *conduct* government. Government was of course to be conducted by the immemorial executive agencies to which Englishmen had grown accustomed, and parliaments were to support those agencies and supply them with money, and to assent to such laws as might be necessary to strengthen the government or regulate the affairs of the country, public or private. Their function was common counsel; their standard of action the ancient understandings of a constitutional system, — a system based on understandings, written or implicit in the experiences and principles of English life. They were expected to give their assent where those understandings were served, and to withhold it where they were disregarded. They were to voice the conscience of the nation in the presence of government and the exercise of authority.

To recall the history is to recall the fundamental conception of the whole process, and to understand our own institutions as they cannot be understood in any other way. It was only by a very slow and round-about development that representative assemblies — at any rate that the English representative assembly, which is the type of all the rest — came to possess or exercise the right to make laws. Many a generation went by before it was supposed that parliament had anything to do with the laws except to give its assent to them or withhold it when new enactments were submitted to it from the king. In the course of time it found only too often that changes in the law were submitted to it in vague general terms and then, after its assent had been given, were formulated and enforced in terms which gave them another scope and color; and such practices led the leaders of the Commons at last to insist that laws should be submitted to them in the full form and statement in which they were to be enforced. It was an easy step from that to the insistence that formulations which did not suit them should be changed, — an easy step to amendment; but it was a step they were long in taking, and even after they had taken it, they suffered the king's officers to formulate the amendment, and often found themselves again cheated, their real purpose defeated by the terms in which it was made. Even so, it was a long time before they undertook to draft 'bills' or proposals of their own, and a longer time still before it became settled practice to have the exact wording of every law submitted first to the debate and choice of parliament. To this day the legislation of parliament in all important matters comes to it on the proposal of the ministers of the crown and is formulated by the law officers of the government. Modern English ministries are in effect merely committees of the House of Commons, made and unmade as parties shift and majorities change; but parliament is still in all its larger aspects the grand assize of the nation, assembled not to originate business, but to apprise the government of what the nation wishes.

Our own legislatures were of the same character and origin. Their liberties and functions grew by similar processes, upon similar understandings, out of the precedents and practices of colonial laws and charters and the circumstances of the age and place. There is a passage in Burke which interprets their growth and character with perfect historical insight, as bodies which had grown, almost insensibly, upon the model of parliament itself. He uttered it as part of his defense of American self-government against the encroachment of parliament, and no one writing in a cooler age can improve upon its analysis.

It is plain that parliaments, that representative bodies, free to criticize not only but acting with independence, uttering the voice of those who are governed, and enjoying such authority as no king or president or officer of any kind may question or gainsay, constitute an indispensable part of the institutional make-up of a constitutional government.  We sometimes attach a very artificial significance to the word 'institution.'  Speaking in the terms of history, and particularly of political history, an institution is merely an established practice, an habitual method of dealing with the circumstances of life or the business of government.  There may be firmly established institutions of which the law knows nothing.  In casting about for a satisfactory way in which to nominate candidates for the office of President of the United States, for instance, our party leaders devised the national nominating convention, and it has become one of our institutions, though neither the constitution nor any statute knows anything of it. And so the growth of constitutional government has been the growth of institutions, of practices, of methods of perfecting the delicate business of maintaining an understanding between those who conduct the government and those who submit to it. ¹ The object of constitutional government is to bring the active, planning will of each part of the government into accord with the prevailing popular thought and need, and thus make it an impartial instrument of symmetrical national development;  and to give to the operation of the government thus shaped under the influence of opinion and adjusted to the general interest both stability and an incorruptible efficacy.   Whatever institutions, whatever practices serve these ends, are necessary to such a system:  those which do not, or which serve it imperfectly, should be dispensed with or bettered. And it may be said that the history of constitutional government has been an experimental search for the best means by which to effect these nice adjustments.

The modern development of the functions of representative assemblies has been in many ways inconsistent with

the real origins and purposes of the practices or institutions in which they had their rise and justification.  We
now regard them, not as bodies assembled to consult with
the government in order to apprise it of the opinion of
the nation with regard to what the government is planning
or doing, not as bodies outside the government set to criticize, restrain, and guide it, but as themselves parts of the
government, its originating, law-*making* parts.  What used
to be called the Government, we now speak of only as
the 'Executive,' and regard as little more than an instrumentality for carrying into effect the laws which our
representative assemblies originate.  Our laws abound in
the most minute administrative details, prescribe the duties
of executive officers and the method by which statutes are
to be put into practice with the utmost particularity, and
all the reins of government seem to have fallen to those
who were once only its censors.  It is, of course, a necessary inference from even the most superficial analysis of
constitutional government that under it those who administer the law and direct the policy of the nation in its
field of action shall be strictly subject to the laws, must
observe the prescribed methods and understandings of the
system very precisely; but it is by no means a necessary
inference that they shall be in leading strings and shall be
reduced to be the mere ministerial agents of a representative
assembly; and the inconveniences and anomalies of this
new practice and conception in the use of assemblies will,
many of them, become manifest enough in our subsequent
examination of our government in its practical operations.

To inquire into such matters is to make intimate approach
to the very essence of constitutional government; but we
approach that essence still more intimately when we turn

from the community, from the nation, and from the assembly which represents it, to the individual. No doubt a great deal of nonsense has been talked about the inalienable rights of the individual, and a great deal that was mere vague sentiment and pleasing speculation has been put forward as fundamental principle. The rights of man are easy to discourse of, may be very pleasingly magnified in the sentences of such constitutions as it used to satisfy the revolutionary ardor of French leaders to draw up and affect to put into operation; but they are infinitely hard to translate into practice. Such theories are never 'law,' no matter what the name or the formal authority of the document in which they are embodied. Only that is 'law' which can be executed, and the abstract rights of man are singularly difficult of execution. None the less, vague talk and ineffectual theory though there be, the individual is indisputably the original, the first fact of liberty. Nations are made up of individuals, and the dealings of government with individuals are the ultimate and perfect test of its constitutional character. A man is not free through representative assemblies, he is free in his own action, in his own dealings with the persons and powers about him, or he is not free at all. There is no such thing as corporate liberty. Liberty belongs to the individual, or it does not exist.

And so the instrumentalities through which individuals are afforded protection against the injustice or the unwarranted exactions of government are central to the whole structure of a constitutional system. From the very outset in modern constitutional history until now it has invariably been recognized as one of the essentials of constitutional government that the individual should be provided with some tribunal to which he could resort with the confident expectation that he should find justice there, — not only justice as against other individuals who had disregarded his rights or sought to disregard them, but also justice against the government itself, a perfect protection against all violations of law. Constitutional government is *par excellence* a government of law.

I am not repeating the famous sentence of the Massachusetts Bill of Rights, "to the end that this may be a government of laws and not of men." There never was such a government. Constitute them how you will, governments are always governments of men, and no part of any government is better than the men to whom that part is intrusted. The gauge of excellence is not the law under which officers act, but the conscience and intelligence with which they apply it, if they apply it at all. And the courts do not escape the rule. So far as the individual is concerned, a constitutional government is as good as its courts; no better, no worse. Its laws are only its professions. It keeps its promises, or does not keep them, in its courts. For the individual, therefore, who stands at the centre of every definition of liberty, the struggle for constitutional government is a struggle for good laws, indeed, but also for intelligent, independent, and impartial courts. Not only is it necessary that the people should be spoken for in the conduct of the government by an assembly truly representative of them; that only such laws should be made or should be suffered to remain in force as effect the best regulation of the national life; and that the administration should be subject to the laws. It is also necessary that there should be a judiciary endowed with substantial and independent powers and secure against all corrupting or perverting

c

influences; secure, also, against the arbitrary authority of the administrative heads of the government.

Indeed there is a sense in which it may be said that the whole efficacy and reality of constitutional government resides in its courts. Our definition of liberty is that it is the best practicable adjustment between the powers of the government and the privileges of the individual; and liberty is the object of constitutional government. The ultimate and characteristic object of a constitutional system is not to effect the best possible adjustment between the government and the community, but the best possible adjustment between the government and the individual; for liberty is individual, not communal. Throughout English history, throughout all the processes which have given us constitutional government as the modern world knows it, those who strove to restrain or to moralize government have perceived that the whole reality of the change must find its expression in the opportunity of the individual to resort for the vindication of his rights to a tribunal which was neither government nor community, but an umpire and judge between them, or rather between government and the man himself, claiming rights to which he was entitled under the general understanding.

Nothing in connection with the development of constitutional government is more remarkable, nothing commends itself more to the understanding of those who perceive the real bases of human dignity and capacity, than the way in which it has exalted the individual, and not only exalted him, but at the same time thrown him upon his own resources, as if it honored him enough to release him from leading strings and trust him to see and seek his own rights. The theory of English and American law is that no man must look to have the government take care of him, but that every man must take care of himself, the government providing the means and making them as excellent as may be, in order that there may be no breach of the peace and that everything may be done, so far as possible, with decency and in order, but never itself taking the initiative, never of its own motion intervening, only standing ready to help when called on. Such an attitude presupposes both intelligence and independence of spirit on the part of the individual: such a system elicits intelligence and creates independence of spirit. The individual must seek his court and must know his remedy, and under such a compulsion he will undertake to do both. The stimulation of such requirements is all that he needs, in addition to his own impulses and desires, to give him the attitude and habit of a free man; and the government set over such men must look to see that it have authority for every act it ventures upon.

It further emphasizes this view and purpose of our law, that no peculiar dignity or sanctity attaches amongst us to any officer of government. The theory of our law is that an officer is an officer only so long as he acts within his powers; that when he transcends his authority he ceases to be an officer and is only a private individual, subject to be sued and punished for his offense. An officer who makes a false arrest without warrant is liable to civil suit for damages and to criminal prosecution for assault. He has stepped out of the ranks of public officers, represents nobody but himself, and is merely committing a private wrong. That is the explicit principle of American law not only, but of English law also: the American practice is derived from the English. It is a logical, matter-of-course inference of the constitutional system: representatives of government have no authority except such as they derive from the law, from the regulations agreed on between the government and those who are to be governed. Whoever disregards the limits of the law transgresses the very fundamental presumptions of the system and becomes merely a lawbreaker, enjoying no privilege or exemption. Such a principle in effect repeats the understanding of Runnymede: 'Here is this charter; sign it and observe it, and you are our king; refuse to sign it, violate or ignore it, and you are not our king, but a man without kingly authority who has done us wrong, and we are your enemies and shall seek redress.' It is the same understanding from the king at the top to the constable at the bottom.

It remains only to note what may be called the atmosphere of constitutional government. It is the atmosphere of opinion. Opinion is, of course, the atmosphere of every government, whatever its forms and powers: governments are contrasted with one another only by the degree and manner in which opinion affects them. There is nowhere any such thing as a literally absolute government. The veriest despot is a creature of circumstances, and the most important circumstance of all, whether he is conscious of adjusting himself to it or not, is the disposition of those about him to obey him or to defy him. Certain things are definitely expected of him: there are certain privileges which he must always respect, certain expectations of caste and of rank which he must always punctiliously regard. Above all there is the great body of habit, the habitual frame of the life in which his own people have been formed, which he would throw himself against in vain. The boundaries of his authority lie where he finds the limits of his subjects' willingness or ability to obey him. They cannot obey him if he seek to force upon them rules too strange to their habit: they will not know how, and their spirits will revolt. They will not obey him if he outrage them by too gross a violation of the understandings which they have come to regard as sacred and of the very essence of their life and happiness. The difference between a constitutional system and an unconstitutional is that in a constitutional system the requirements of opinion are clearly formulated and understood, while in an unconstitutional they are vague and conjectural. The unconstitutional ruler has to guess where his subjects will call a halt upon him, and experiment at the hazard of his throne and head; the constitutional ruler definitely knows the limits which he must not transgress and is safe in his authority so long as he does not overstep them.

But there is this radical difference between the opinion which limits the power of an unconstitutional ruler and that which limits the powers of a constitutional government: that the one is unorganized opinion, the other organized; the one hardly more than an impatient stir at any disturbance of tradition or of habit, the other a quick concert of thought, uttered by those who know how to guide both counsel and action. Indeed, there has seldom been in the case of a despotic government anything that really corresponded with what in constitutional government is known as public opinion. The wit who described the government of France as despotism tempered by epigram was really formulating one of the approaches to constitutional government. When opinion spoken in the salon begins to be a definite organ of criticism, when criticism has become concerted and powerful enough and sufficiently mixed with the passion of action to serve from time to time as a modifying, guiding, and controlling force, the development of constitutional government has begun.

It is therefore peculiarly true of constitutional government that its atmosphere is opinion, the air from which it takes its breath and vigor. The underlying understandings of a constitutional system are modified from age to age by changes of life and circumstance and corresponding alterations of opinion. It does not remain fixed in any unchanging form, but grows with the growth and is altered with the change of the nation's needs and purposes. The constitution of England, the original and typical constitutional government of the world, is unwritten except for its statement of individual right and privilege in Magna Carta, in the Bill of Rights, and in the Petition of Right; is, in other words, only a body of very definite opinion, except for occasional definitions of statute here and there. Its substance is the thought and habit of the nation, its conscious expectations and preferences; and around even a written constitution there grows up a body of practices which have no formal recognition or sanction in the written law, which even modify the written stipulations of the system in many subtle ways and become the instrument of opinion in effecting a slow transformation. If it were not so, the written document would become too stiff a garment for the living thing.

It is in this sense that institutions are the creatures of opinion. Their breath and vigor goes out of them when they cease to be sustained by the conscious or habitual preference of the people whose practice has created them; and new institutions take their place when once that practice is altered. That is what gives dignity to citizenship among a free people.    Every man's thought is part of the vital substance of its institutions.    With the change of his thought, institutions themselves may change.    That is what constitutes citizenship so responsible and solemn a thing.    Every man in a free country is, as it were, put upon his honor to be the kind of man such a polity supposes its citizens to be: a man with his thought upon the general welfare, his interest consciously linked with the interests of his fellow-citizens, his sense of duty broadened to the scope of public affairs.    Every generation in a free state realizes that the perpetuation of its institutions depends upon the thought and disposition of the generations which are to follow, and busies itself to hand the impulse and the conception on by careful processes of education, stamping its thought upon young men, seeking to make its own frame of mind permanent.    Old phrases spring to new significance as one's thought clears in such matters.    "Eternal vigilance is the price of liberty."    The threadbare phrase seems new stuff when we wear it on our understandings.    The vigilance of intelligently directed opinion is indeed the very soil of liberty and of all the enlightened institutions meant to sustain it.    And that will always be the freest country in which enlightened opinion abounds, in which to plant the practices of government.    It is of the essence of a constitutional system that its people should think straight, maintain a consistent purpose, look before and after, and make their lives the image of their thoughts.

We may summarize our view of constitutional government by saying that its ultimate and essential objects are:

1st.    To bring the active and planning will of each part of the government into accord with the prevailing popular thought and need, in order that government may be the impartial instrument of a symmetrical national development;

2d. To give to the law thus formulated under the influence of opinion and adjusted to the general interest both stability and an incorruptible efficacy;

3d. To put into the hands of every individual, without favor or discrimination, the means of enforcing the understandings of the law alike with regard to himself and with regard to the operations of government, the means of challenging every illegal act that touches him.

And that, accordingly, the essential elements and institutions of a constitutional system are: —

1st. A more or less complete and particular formulation of the rights of individual liberty, — that is, the rights of the individual against the community or its government, — such as is contained in Magna Carta and in the Bills of Rights attached to our constitutions;

2d. An assembly, representative of the community or of the people, and not of the government: a body set to criticize, restrain, and control the government;

3d. A government or executive subject to the laws, and .

4th. A judiciary with substantial and independent powers, secure against all corrupting or perverting influences; secure, also, against the arbitrary authority of the government itself.

## II

### THE PLACE OF THE UNITED STATES IN CONSTITUTIONAL DEVELOPMENT

· It will greatly enrich our conception of what a constitutional government is to look a little farther into its history. The government of the United States came into existence at a very interesting turning-point in that history, and will lie very much more open to our analysis if we pause before we go farther to examine the circumstances of its origin. Historical excursions are sometimes tedious enough, but the matter we handle cannot be made vital until it is given its true historical setting.

Evidently, if a constitutional government is a government conducted on the basis of a definite understanding between those who administer it and those who obey it, there can be no constitutional government unless there be a community to sustain and develop it, — unless the nation, whose instrument it is, is conscious of common interests and can form common purposes. A people not conscious of any unity, inorganic, unthoughtful, without concert of action, can manifestly neither form nor sustain a constitutional system. The lethargy of an unawakened consciousness is upon them, the helplessness of unformed purpose. They can form no common judgment; they can conceive no common end; they can contrive no common measures. Nothing but a community can have a

25

constitutional form of government, and if a nation has not become a community, it cannot have that sort of polity. It is necessary at the very outset of our analysis, therefore, that we should form a very definite conception of what a community is, and should ask ourselves very frankly whether the United States can be regarded as a community or not. Only in that way can we determine the place of the United States in constitutional development; and only practical historical tests will answer either the one question or the other.

The word 'community' is often upon our lips, but seldom receives any clear definition in our thoughts. If we should examine our implicit assumptions with regard to it, I suppose that we should agree in saying that no body of people could constitute a community in any true or practical sense who did not have a distinct consciousness of common ties and interests, a common manner and standard of life and conduct, and a practised habit of union and concerted action in whatever affected it as a whole. It is in this understanding of the term that we speak when we say that only a community can have a constitutional government. No body of people which is not clearly conscious of common interests and of common standards of life and happiness can come to any satisfactory agreement with its government, and no people which has not a habit of union and concerted action in regard to its affairs could secure itself against the breach of such an agreement if it existed. A people must have the impulse and must find the means to express itself in institutions if it is to have a constitutional system.

I should be at a loss to define what I mean by a common political consciousness, but fortunately it does not need

definition. What it is is part of the imaginative conception of every one whose mind has traveled at all in the
realms of history and of social experience. With every
one of us it is an idea which is as definite as it is subtle
and complex. We know that that body of persons is
not a community along whose blood the same events do
not send the same thrill, upon whose purposes and upon
whose consciousness the same events do not make the
same impression, and who are not capable, at every turn
in their affairs, of forming resolutions and executing measures which will meet the exigency. You remember those
fine sentences of De Tocqueville's with regard to the forma-
tion of our own government, in which he speaks with
admiring wonder of the calm and self-reliant way in which
the people of the colonies turned a critical eye upon themselves, detected, as if they looked not upon their own
institutions but upon those of others, the serious defects
of their political system, and remedied them "without
having drawn a tear or a drop of blood from mankind."
In proportion as they had a common consciousness with
regard to their affairs, they were capable of handling them
and of setting up a government which should last. The
historical circumstances which explain the capacity of
the colonists explain also the character of the government
of the United States and make plain its place in constitutional development. How was the United States made
a community? How far and in what matters was its
consciousness as a community developed? How have
its institutions responded to that development, and how
do they now stand related to it? These are the questions
whose answers may be expected to give us light upon our
whole inquiry.

Looked at from the point of view of our present study, government may be said to have passed, roughly speaking, through four stages and forms of development: a first stage in which the government was master, the people veritable subjects; a second in which the government, ceasing to be master by virtue of sheer force and unquestioned authority, remained master by virtue of its insight and sagacity, its readiness and fitness to lead; a third in which both sorts of mastery failed it and it found itself face to face with leaders of the people who were bent upon controlling it, a period of deep agitation and full of the signs of change; and a fourth in which the leaders of the people themselves became the government, and the development was complete.

Government may be said to have been master both in the early Germanic feudal nation which occupied the European field after the break-up of the Roman Empire and in the developed feudal nation in which a monarch like Louis XIV could say with almost literal truth, *L'état c'est moi;* and also in the nations which have been subjugated by some military race or class, conquering them from without and retaining their hold upon them by organized force, as in China and Russia. Such governments represent always a stage of social development: the stage at which the people governed are conscious of no community of interest, no possible concert of action amongst them; do not feel themselves a single body or stir with any common purpose; have not formed the idea of an interest of their own opposed to the interest of the government, or, if they have begun vaguely to form it, know no means of making their separate wish known or effective: a people dumb and without knowledge of speech in such matters. A

people may or may not linger at this stage.  The nation
which is most likely to linger until it stagnates is the caste
nation, caught in a crust of custom which it is almost
impossible to break or even to alter, unless some irresistible
force from without break and destroy it, as the force of
the western nations has so ruthlessly broken the ancient
forms of Chinese life.  The military nation is quite sure
to change very rapidly: it is too full of stir and force to
retain its first forms or stand still at one stage of development; and the monarch of the modern state to which the
feudal state gave birth is more apt than another to attempt
progress and development, as the kings of modern Europe
did.  The population which is ruled by a limited class
who are its conquerors is apt, if we may judge by the case
of Russia, to stand still until the polity rots.

The stagnation of peoples is very hard for us to think
of in our modern western world, but it has none the less
been the rule, not the exception, as Mr. Bagehot pointed
out in that illuminating book, "Physics and Politics."
If we reckon by numerical majorities, the rule has been
stagnation; much the greater part of the population of
the world has been caught fast in a crust of custom or in
an iron net of military rule, and has known no political
progress.  Even those peoples who have struggled toward
the light and sought emancipation from the trammels of
too much government have moved with painful slowness
toward their goal, so long as there were none of those
quick means of concerting thought and action which have
been supplied us in the telegraph, the railway, and
the cheapened printing press.  Without these instrumentalities it is to be doubted whether we could ever have
spread a single free state over the spaces of a great con-

tinent, as we have done in America, where there were already people accustomed to do as they pleased and to act upon their own initiative. Concerted action does not come by impulse but by practice, by the slow schooling of experience, chiefly by the schooling of repeated failures. A common purpose can be formed only by the slow processes of common counsel, until our own day a thing infinitely tedious and difficult. Many a long age stretches between the moment when a nation begins to awaken to the consciousness that it has common ties and a common interest as against a too masterful and selfish government and the triumphant moment when it sees its own chosen leaders in actual control of its law and policy. The first stirrings of that consciousness change the face of affairs and usher in the second stage of development of which I have spoken; and from it governments that have sagacity enough to respond take their golden opportunity to lead.

It is then that government finds itself checked by the beginnings of independent action on the part of the nation, irregular and imperfectly organized it may be, but definite and significant enough to demand the consideration and often to modify the course of those who rule, lest government should fail of being obeyed and should jeopard civil order, if not its own authority and security. It was so in England in the time of Elizabeth. Parliaments had not yet obtained any place of command. They were consulted when the monarch pleased, and not oftener. Their counsels restrained, but did not govern. The will of the monarch was sometimes stronger than the understandings of the constitution. Opinion had not come to its full stature; authority still loomed large and imperative in every ordinary matter of state. But England was astir as she never had been before. In the old days she had been at the back of Europe; now she was at her front. The doors of the East had been closed by the conquests of the Turk; the barrier of his intolerant power was thrown across the old routes of trade out of Europe into the great Orient, and Europe had turned her face about to seek new outlets for her commerce: down the western coasts of Africa and so around the southern capes into the East again, and across the vast Atlantic to the new lands slowly rising to view over sea, — whether in fact a new world or only the old coasts of the East approached from another side mariners or geographers had not yet quite made up their minds. Columbus had turned his adventurous prows straight toward the heart of the seemingly limitless ocean whose mysteries no man before him had dared look into; and England herself, lying at the very gates of that sea, had been quick to send her own sailors in his wake. Englishmen of every rank and fortune began to turn to the sea for adventure and profit, and the sixteenth century saw the little kingdom wake to influences and ambitions she had never felt before. It was a mettlesome race Elizabeth found herself set to govern.

Whether she was conscious that they were not easy to rule and were likely to have minds of their own in matters of government it is not necessary to ask, because she was of the same mettle and spirit as they, a truly representative Englishman, inclined to lead her people in their own temper and quick to see their interests as they saw them. Mr. John Richard Green has said that in her dealings with foreign governments Elizabeth was one of the most accomplished liars of her day, but that she always dealt candidly and truthfully with her own subjects. It was not so much the circumspection of a wise ruler who wishes to retain the confidence of those upon whose obedience he counts for all the vigor of his policy as the instinctive sympathy and quick understanding that naturally exists between persons of the same purpose and breeding.  England came to her full consciousness as a nation in that great day of enterprise and adventure, and Elizabeth was England's suitable embodiment.  Her mastery was the mastery of natural leadership.  Her instinctive knowledge of what was demanded of her shows in nothing better than in her treatment of the great seamen who explored the long coasts of the new world and lifted treasure from every Spanish fleet they could find.  She gave them their commissions and asked no inconvenient questions.  So long as they kept troth with her, came to her at her command, executed her purposes when she had need of them, paid reasonable tribute into her treasury, and made all rival seamen respect her power, she freely gave them leave as they wished.  Never in any other age had English energy been so quickened and released: a great ruler made great subjects.

There were dark sides enough to the picture.  There were phases of English life to which there is not here time to turn in which the royal authority showed sinister and without true insight into either the rights or the interests of the kingdom, — monopolies, illegal exactions, private favors, a thousand irregularities of power, — but that was nothing new; while it was a new thing to have a monarch who, at any rate in all large matters, understood her people and lent her sagacity to the task of leading and stimulating them.  In the nick of time, when they most needed a leader, she gave them one in her own person, — a foolish woman but a great statesman.

We have another example of the same thing in a very different age in the leadership of Frederick the Great of Prussia. The Prussia of the middle of the eighteenth century was in almost no respect like the England of the middle of the sixteenth. Frederick, when he came to lead and develop Prussia, had but just put her together out of pieces swept under his single rule by the processes of war. Neither is there any close similarity between the characters of Frederick and Elizabeth. They resembled one another in character no more than any strong and masterful man who was born a statesman resembles any masterful woman born a statesman. But Frederick did for Prussia more than Elizabeth did for England. He first made it a compact and potentially powerful kingdom, and then himself called it into consciousness. Elizabeth gave expression in her own person and gifts to a new nation that had been born and would have been born whether she had lived to rule it or not; Frederick called his kingdom into life and gave it the leadership of an awakening; and he did so on the eve of the modern time, as peoples were everywhere beginning to awake, and so affords us an admirable example, as Elizabeth does, of what a government may do by way of leadership, in anticipation of the day when the people will find sympathetic leaders for themselves if their rulers fail to supply them.

Frederick probably did more for Prussia than she could have done for herself under leaders of her own choosing. He saw her and understood her as a whole. She was in a sense of his own making. He wished her to have internal development rather because he wished her to be strong among the states of Europe than because he wished to see her strength and prosperity increase as a statesman

D

would in times when he was sure of peace; desired her economic enlargement chiefly because he wished his treasury to be full, his kingdom's resources sufficient for any long-drawn contest of arms that might be necessary with the rivals about him; and it must be said that he treated his subjects like servants rather than like citizens of a great state. But under all his purpose of aggrandizement and of international supremacy there lay a real sympathy with his people, a real insight into their interests and necessities, a real capacity to interpret and guide them. He was a leader as well as a master, and his rule gave Prussia such prestige as England had had in the times of the great Elizabeth. He led a new nation out on to the stage of Europe and made it ready for at any rate the initial stages of self-government, by giving it the self-consciousness and regard for its own interests which come of enterprise. A living people needs not a master but a leader.

Leaders like Frederick and Elizabeth are, of course, self-constituted, and the great statesmen whom such rulers draw into their counsels are, of course, of their own, not of the nation's, choosing. The nation is supplied with leaders, does not find them. It is too early for it to find them; it has not learned the way. Such a form and stage of government, the second on our list, represents a stage of political development, as the first of which I spoke represents a stage of social development. When a government is master and the people its unquestioned subjects, society is asleep, is unformed, inorganic, without self-consciousness, and without knowledge of its own interests and power. What is lacking is the birth of a national consciousness and self-knowledge. When the second stage comes the nation has become aware of itself, aware of the drift and significance of its affairs, aware in some degree of its rôle and ambition among the nations; but it has not yet learned to choose its own leaders. It has had the social development necessary to bring it to the threshold of fully developed constitutional arrangements, but not the political development. It has not yet learned how to express itself in men thrust forward out of its own ranks or how to form such common resolutions and contrive such common counsels as would give leaders of its own choice a definite program of action, even if it could choose them. Of course the England of the time of Elizabeth had already had a political development such as Prussia knew nothing of in Frederick's day. Her parliament lay ready to her hand, a true representative assembly, to be turned to any use of common counsel or concerted action she might wish; while Prussia had nothing but her king and a dependent bureaucracy which he had created. In England the full machinery of constitutional government as it were lay dormant, not put to its final uses because Elizabeth saved her people the trouble and by her own leadership postponed the final developments of constitutional government until the weak Stuarts who followed her should make the authority to which she had given such dignity and prestige at last ridiculous and intolerable.

Nations will pass from such a stage of political development by steady transition, change by change, into those arrangements whereby the freely chosen leaders of the people themselves at last assume control of the government, only if, while their hereditary rulers thus by natural genius lead them, a serviceable machinery of constitutional action exist or be formed by means of which the transition can be effected. This was the case in England, but not in Prussia. In England there were both parliament and a self-governing country gentry habituated to affairs. In Prussia there was nothing but a dependent bureaucracy neither derived from the people nor capable of independent initiative in their interest.

And yet, whether there be the requisite machinery at hand or not, an awakened modern nation cannot long stand still at the stage where its affairs are managed without its direct institutional participation and assent. Things cannot long stand still where a whole arrangement depends upon the temper and insight of rulers whose authority is independent of the people's choice, or upon an international situation and the social and economic condition of the country. National conditions are not often for long so simple or so comprehensible that a government not derived from the people can retain the sympathetic comprehension necessary to leadership. Moreover, the times which immediately followed the exceptional reigns of Frederick and Elizabeth were times when deep common convictions began to stir amidst all ranks and kinds of men; the convictions of the great Protestant Reformation and of the fateful French Revolution, the two great epochs when plain men, who had hitherto taken little heed of affairs either in church or state, were aroused to know themselves and their rights, alike of conscience and of political recognition. Such awakenings of the minds and hearts of whole peoples produced leaders as of course. Great passions, when they run through a whole population, inevitably find a great spokesman. A people cannot remain dumb which is moved by profound impulses of conviction; and when spokesmen and leaders are found, effective concert of action seems to follow as naturally. Men spring together for common action under a common impulse which has taken hold upon their very natures, and governments presently find that they have those to reckon with who know not only what they want, but also the most effective means of making governments uncomfortable until they get it. Governments find themselves, in short, in the presence of *Agitation*, of systematic movements of opinion which do not merely flare up in spasmodic flame and then die down again, but burn with an accumulating ardor which can be checked and extinguished only by removing the grievances and abolishing the unacceptable institutions which are its fuel. Casual discontent can be allayed, but agitation fixed upon conviction cannot be. To fight it is merely to augment its force. It burns irrepressibly in every public assembly; quiet it there, and it gathers head at street corners; drive it thence, and it smoulders in private dwellings, in social gatherings, in every covert of talk, only to break forth more violently than ever because denied vent and air. It must be reckoned with, and to reckon with it is to set up a new understanding between governors and governed, to consent to new practices which are new institutions, to enter the fourth stage, which leads to the full development of constitutional rule.

The third stage of the matter, the stage of agitation, has often been a long one and a sad one. Governments have been very resourceful in parrying agitation, in diverting it, in seeming to yield to it and then cheating it of its objects, in tiring it out or evading it; and where men of conviction lack any permanent instrument, like the English parliament, upon which to centre their efforts, in which to find some unquestionable legal forum where to bring the pressure of their purposes constantly to bear on the government, agitation may often fail entirely for generations together, its flame smothered or scattered from age to age. But the end, whether it come soon or late, is quite certain to be always the same. In one nation in one form, in another in another, but wherever conviction is awakened and serious purpose results from it, this at last happens: that the people's leaders will themselves take control of the government as they have done in England, in Switzerland, in America, in France, in Scandinavia, and in Italy, and as they will yet do in every other country whose polity fulfils the promise of the modern time.

We are so accustomed to agitation, to absolutely free, outspoken argument for change, to an unrestrained criticism of men and measures carried almost to the point of licence, that to us it seems a normal, harmless part of the familiar processes of popular government. We have learned that it is pent-up feelings that are dangerous, whispered purposes that are revolutionary, covert follies that warp and poison the mind; that the wisest thing to do with a fool is to encourage him to hire a hall and discourse to his fellow citizens. Nothing chills nonsense like exposure to the air; nothing dispels folly like its publication; nothing so eases the machine as the safety valve. Agitation is certainly of the essence of a constitutional system, but those who exercise authority under a non-constitutional system fear its impact with a constant dread and try by every possible means to check and kill it, partly no doubt because they know that agitation is dangerous to arrangements which are unreasonable, and non-constitutional rule is highly unreasonable in countries whose people can express such common thoughts and contrive such concert of action as make agitation formidable.  But there is always another reason why rulers so circumstanced should instinctively fear agitation.  Agitation is unquestionably very dangerous in countries where there are no institutions — no parliaments, councils, occasional assemblies even — in which opinion may legitimately and with the sanction of law transmute itself into action.  Speech is not the only vent opinion needs; it needs also the satisfactions of action.

And action is very sobering to opinion.  It is one thing to advocate reforms; it is quite another to formulate them. Many an ardent and burdensome reformer would be silenced and put to better thinking if he were obliged to express his reform in the exact words of a workable statute; and many a statute which amateurs may think eminently workable turns out impossible of execution.  One of the things which is most instructive to the practical student of our own government is the tendency of our legislatures, both state and federal, to enact impracticable laws.  Our legislatures do not have to put their own enactments into execution.  The chairmen of their committees may often be as absolute tyros in the actual business of government as the members of reform clubs whom they have contemptuously dubbed theorists; and their own theories of what ought to be done do not cease to be theories because expressed in documents introduced by an enacting clause. They sometimes escape the blame attaching to the failure of the laws they frame by adroitly putting it off on the executive officers of the government, representing them as not in sympathy with the enactment and disinclined to give it a full or honest trial in practice; but many a statute is still-born, and agitation which results in still-births is harmless.  The agitators have had their way, and nothing has happened. Action has released the pent-up energy, and no harm has been done. But under non-constitutional forms of government no vent of action is supplied, and a sort of fury of helplessness may ensue whose mad issue may be the very destruction of government itself.

When the fourth and final stage of constitutional development is reached, when a people has gained so definite a consciousness of its own interests and of its own political force, has grown so accustomed to forming its own opinions and following its own leaders that it becomes natural and, indeed, inevitable, that its leaders should themselves take charge of the government and direct it, one or other of two forms of government may result: the parliamentary English form or the American form, which Mr. Bagehot has, not very happily, perhaps, called the "presidential." Under the parliamentary form of government the people's recognized leaders for the time being, that is, the leaders of the political party which for the time commands a majority in the popular house of parliament, are both heads of the executive and guides of the legislature. They both conduct government and suggest legislation. All the chief measures of a parliamentary session originate with them, and they are under the sobering necessity of putting into successful execution the laws they propose. Under our own system the people as a whole consciously take part in the choice of but one man, the President, and he is not expected to lead Congress, but only to assent to or dissent from the laws it seeks to enact and to put those which receive his signature or are passed over his veto into execution; while Congress is guided by men whom the nation may or may not have regarded as its leaders and who are preferred to places of leadership in the House and Senate by processes which those houses have themselves devised. The President may be of one party and the houses of Congress of the other. The executive and legislature are not necessarily united in counsel with us as they are in England.

Moreover, what is vastly more important in contrasting our system with others, we have not concentrated our constitutional arrangements in the federal government. We have multiplied our constitutional governments by the number of our states, and have set up in each commonwealth of a vast union of states a separate constitutional government to which is intrusted the regulation of all the ordinary relations of citizens to each other: their property rights, their family relations, their rights of contract, their relations as employer and employed, their suits at law, and their criminal liabilities. The federal government has only the regulation of those matters in which there is manifestly and of necessity a common interest, and for the rest constitutional government is put into commission among forty odd commonwealths.

Both arrangements, the partial separation of the executive from the legislature in the federal government and the parceling out of constitutional powers among the states, mark the historical stage alike of our own development and of the development of constitutional government on the other side of the water at which the government of the United States came into existence. In the state governments there is the same partial separation of legislature and executive that is characteristic of the federal government, because the constitutions of the states were formulated at the same time that the government of the Union was formulated. That is the characteristic they derive from the period in which they originated. The dispersion of constitutional powers among the states originated in circumstances peculiar to America. Switzerland, it is true, has a similar union and division; but though the results in Switzerland are very similar to the results in America, the circumstances of origin and formulation were very different in the two countries. Both peculiarities of our system yield upon analysis very interesting conclusions with regard to the nature and the characteristic processes of constitutional government.

The Constitution of the United States, as framed by the constitutional convention of 1787, was intended to be a copy of the government of England, with such changes as seemed to our own statesmen necessary to safeguard the people of America against the particular sorts of prerogative and power that had worked them harm in their dealings with the government of the mother country over sea. But the government of England was then in a process of transition from an older to a newer form of the constitutional series and had not advanced far enough in the transformation to disclose its real character. Even in our own day, when English ministries are acknowledged to be mere committees of the majority in the House of Commons, the king chooses the ministers. At least such is the legal fiction. But it is not so in fact. It is merely a form. He is obliged to select those of whom the majority in the House of Commons approves. Indeed, he merely calls on the leader of that majority to form a ministry and leaves it to him to say whom the other ministers shall be. He can follow his own judgment in the choice only in the very exceptional case where no one man looms conspicuously first among the leaders of the Commons and the majority in the House is not itself certain of its preference. But

when the Constitution of the United States was framed,
what is now a form was a reality. The choice of the king
was a very real one. He as often as possible chose ministers to his own mind. It is true that ever since the Revolution of 1688 it had generally been necessary for him to
select men whom the Commons would follow, against
whom they would at least not revolt; but the suffrage for
members of parliament was then so disposed that the king
and a small group of peers could generally determine the
majority in the House of Commons by one sort of influence
or another. The king could even on occasion turn his pliant
majority over from one minister to another of opposite
views when the policy of the crown changed or yielded to
pressure. And so the change that was steadily coming
upon the whole composition of the government was obscured. The members of the constitutional convention of
1787 naturally enough thought of the king as the executive,
a power separate from parliament not only but often in
contest with it, and did not see that influences were already
working throughout the system which were to transmute
the ministry, so soon as the suffrage should be reformed
and parliament should become truly representative of the
nation, into a committee of the Commons of which the king
should have formal appointment but not real choice, and
which should itself constitute the working executive of the
country, making choice, in the king's stead, of every step
of regulation or policy. The President created by our
Constitution was conceived upon the model of what it
was thought the king should have been under the older
practice of the English constitution, at the very time when
English theory and practice alike were changing and direct
party government by the legislative leaders of the people

was actually in course of being set up. We were fixed fast, in respect of the presidential office, at the stage of constitutional development which England was leaving for forms simpler and still more advanced.

Our reasons for having a group of constitutional governments united in a federal constitutional system were not reasons of theory, but reasons of fact. The thirteen little commonwealths which had drawn together in confederation to fight out the war for independence had attained to a growth and character which had made veritable states of them. No merging of them as a single state under one government was possible or conceivable. It was a triumph of statesmanship to unite them by the bonds of a real federal state which was not a mere loosely joined confederation like that which had barely held together long enough to finish the war. A strong sense of community of interest had grown up among the colonies as they fought the French and Indians and struggled for independence; they were resolved to have a common life and stand together for common objects; were keenly aware that separately they could not survive the struggle for political existence which must certainly rise out of their own rivalries and the covetous attacks of foreign powers; and were determined that their common government should be at least strong enough to unite them firmly as a nation. But the catalogue of common interests, the list of powers they must for their own sakes concede to their common government, did not bulk very big in their thoughts. Their state governments were their chief governments, their everyday, essential, intimate, vital instruments of social order and political action. For a little while they looked upon the new federal organization as an experiment, and thought it likely it might not last. Men of first-rate capacity and high political ambition entered the service of their states readily enough, but looked askance upon offers of federal office. Only the extraordinary foresight and sagacity of the men who framed and advocated the federal constitution, — only the prevailing force of such men as Washington, and Hamilton, and Madison, — could have secured so compact and strong a central government in the face of the jealousy of local interests. The wonder was not that constitutional power remained "in commission" among the states, but that any central authority capable of rule and command had been got from the jealous politicians of the self-conscious little commonwealths.

That the states survived the union was no political accident. Their separateness did not consist in the mere casual circumstance that they had been settled at different times and their governments as colonies separately chartered by the English kings. Vital social and economic differences existed between them. They could not have been made a real political community by any single constitution, however broadly and wisely conceived, because they were not a community in fact. They were in many respects sharply contrasted in life and interest. Virginia was much more unlike Massachusetts than Massachusetts was unlike England. The Carolinas, with their lumber forests and their rice fields, felt themselves utterly unlike Virginia; and the Middle states, with their mixture of population out of many lands, were unlike both New England and the South. The Middle states, New York, New Jersey, and Pennsylvania, were, indeed, not mere transplantations out of the mother country; they had the mixture of peoples in them which was in the years to come to be characteristic of America. In them rather than in the communities east or south of them lay hidden the prophecy of what America was to be, and they in some subtle way felt the contrast between their own ways and purposes and those of their neighbors very keenly. Constitutional government is based upon common understandings, common interests, common impulses, common habits, and these each of the little commonwealths of the Union had; but in the federal state which they had devised in the Philadelphia convention these things did not yet exist except as regarded the matters of commerce, of coinage, of post-offices and post roads, of piracies and felonies on the high seas, of war and military defense, and of dealings with foreign governments of which so careful a catalogue had been made in the eighth section of the first article of the federal constitution. The states were not one community but many communities, and as such could not have had a single government; were under the necessity of having as many constitutional units as there were actual political divisions. The very complexity of the arrangement was of the essence of practical good sense and showed how true an instinct the leaders of that day had for successful constitutional method.

Our life has undergone radical changes since 1787, and almost every change has operated to draw the nation together, to give it the common consciousness, the common interests, the common standards of conduct, the habit of concerted action, which will eventually impart to it in many more respects the character of a single community. No student of constitutional development can have observed these vital processes without perceiving what their end and consequence will be. The copper threads of the telegraph run unbroken to every nook and corner of the great continent, like the nerves of a single body, transmitting thought and purpose with instant precision. Railways lie in every valley and stretch across every plain. Cheap newspapers make the news of every country-side the news of the nation. Industrial organization knows nothing of state lines, and commerce sweeps from state to state in currents which can hardly be traced for number and intricacy. Ideas, motives, standards of conduct, subtle items of interest, airs from out every region travel with the news, with the passenger on the express train, with the merchant's goods and the farmer's grain. Invisible shuttles of suggestion weave the thoughts and purposes of separate communities together, and a nation which will some day know itself a single community is a-making in the warp and woof of the fabric. The extraordinary way in which the powers of the federal government have been suffered to grow in recent years is evidence enough of the process.

It is a process which has gone forward with a noble dramatic, even epic, majesty, filling the whole stage of the continent with movement. Until 1890 we had always a frontier within the nation; until that year the makers of the census had always been able in drawing their maps to sketch a line somewhere between the older states and the Pacific which marked the front of organized settlement. A hundred years had gone by since the constitution was framed, and throughout all the century the same process of settlement had been going on which marked the first establishment of the colonies. The stages of development within the nation itself varied all the way from communities on the eastern coast which were at length hardly to be distinguished from European communities in their complexity, their variety, their pageantry of life to communities in the West more sharply contrasted with those in the East than Virginia from England in the seventeenth century. To travel from the Atlantic coast to the frontier was like viewing a colossal exhibit illustrative by actual life of all the processes that had made and were making the nation. Since 1890 there has been no traceable frontier; the processes have begun to be intensive rather than extensive. The processes which knit close and unite all fibres into one cloth are now everywhere visible to any one who will look beneath the surface.

It is familiar matter of history that it is this westward expansion, this constant projection of new communities into the West, this never ceasing spread and adaptation of our institutions and our modes of life, that has been the chief instrumentality in giving us national feeling, that has kept our eyes lifted to tasks which had manifest destiny in them, and could be compassed by no merely local agencies. It was the constant making of states that forced upon every generation of statesmen the question whether slavery should be extended or restricted in area until the Civil War answered it forever, and that controversy more than any other called the nation to consciousness and to action. Ours has been for the most part a very businesslike history. Our congressional annals have not been brightened by many picturesque incidents or quickened by many dramatic moments, but there is one debate to which every student turns with the feeling that in it lay the fire of the central dramatic force of all our history. In the debate between Mr. Hayne and Mr. Webster the whole feeling and consciousness of America was changed. Mr.

Hayne had uttered, with singular eloquence and ringing force, the voice of a day that was passing away; Mr. Webster the voice of a day that had come and whose forces were to supersede all others.  There is a sense in which it may almost be said that Mr. Webster that day called a nation into being.  What he said has the immortal quality of words which almost create the thoughts they speak.  The nation lay as it were unconscious of its unity and purpose, and he called it into full consciousness.  It could never again be anything less than what he had said that it was.  It is at such moments and in the mouths of such interpreters that nations spring from age to age in their development.  And in our modern day influences less heated and dramatic than those of the days of the westward movement, influences that operate silent and unobserved in the economic and social changes that are working a great synthesis upon us, are carrying the nationalizing process steadily and irresistibly forward to the same great consummation.

But there are natural limits beyond which such a development cannot go, and our state governments are likely to become, not less, but more vital units in our system as the natural scope and limits of their powers are more clearly and permanently established.  In a great political system like our own, spread abroad over the vast spaces of a various continent, the states are essential.  We are now in the midst of changes whose sweep is so wide that we exaggerate their force and suppose that because they are not checked by state boundaries, and for the time even seem to obscure them, they will eventually obliterate them.  We shall be surprised, when the changes are completed, to find how little they have altered our constitutional machinery.  What they will alter very radically is our national

E

consciousness, our perception of the interests we have in common, and of the principles upon which we must act in dealing with them.  The change will be psychological rather than political, of the spirit of our action rather than of its method.  Undoubtedly the sphere of our national government will be in many important particulars notably enlarged; but it will be in particulars and not in principle, by normal and legitimate alterations of the constitutional understanding and not by any reconstruction of the system.

Not only are the separate and independent powers of the states based upon real economic and social differences between section and section of an enormous country, differences which necessitate adaptations of law and of administrative policy such as only local authorities acting in real independence can intelligently effect; but the states are our great and permanent contribution to constitutional development.  I call them a great contribution because they have given to the understandings upon which constitutional government is based an intimacy and detail, an adjustment to local circumstances, a national diversity, an immediate adaptation to the variety of the people themselves, such as a little country may perhaps dispense with but a great continent cannot.  The development of the United States would have been as impossible without the state governments as the original establishment of our federal system would have been.  They have furnished us with an ideal means of integrating a vast and various population, adapting law to changing and temporary conditions, modulating development, and permanently securing each item of progress.  They have been an incomparable means of sensitive adjustment between popular thought and governmental method, and may yet afford the world itself the model of federation and liberty it may in God's providence come to seek. There can be no reasonable fear that our states will ever be less than they are, the normal constitutional machinery of our legal adjustment. As the federal government grows in scope and power it will grow, not to their curtailment, but only by way of supplementing them and by way of safeguarding those interests, from the first looked forward to by the makers of the Constitution, in which we shall consciously become a single community.

This is not a conclusion got out of sentiment or preference, but out of the necessary inferences of constitutional history. Constitutional government can exist only where there is actual community of interest and of purpose, and cannot, if it be also *self*-government, express the life of any body of people that does not constitute a veritable community. Are the United States a community? In some things, yes; in most things, no. How impossible it is to generalize about the United States! If a foreign acquaintance ask you a question about America, are you not obliged before replying to say, "Which part of America do you refer to?" It would be hard to frame any single generalization which would be true of the whole United States, whether it were social, economic, or political. It is a matter of despair to describe a typical American. Types vary from region to region, and even from state to state. America abounds in the vitality of variety and can be summed up in no formula either of description or of prophecy.

Moreover, she is a country not merely constitutionally governed, but also self-governed. To look upon her and comprehend her is to comprehend the distinction. Self-government is the last, the consummate stage of constitutional development. Peoples which are not yet highly developed, self-conscious communities can be constitutionally governed, as England was before she had got her full character and knowledge of herself, under monarchs who ruled her by their own will, checked but not governed by her parliament; but only communities can govern themselves and dispense with every form of absolute authority. There is profound truth in Sir Henry Maine's remark that the men who colonized America and made its governments, to the admiration of the world, could never have thus masterfully taken charge of their own affairs and combined stability with liberty in the process of absolute self-government if they had not sprung of a race habituated to submit to law and authority, if their fathers had not been the subjects of kings, if the stock of which they came had not served the long apprenticeship of political childhood during which law was law without choice of their own. Self-government is not a mere form of institutions, to be had when desired, if only proper pains be taken. It is a form of character. It follows upon the long discipline which gives a people self-possession, self-mastery, the habit of order and peace and common counsel, and a reverence for law which will not fail when they themselves become the makers of law: the steadiness and self-control of political maturity. And these things cannot be had without long discipline.

The distinction is of vital concern to us in respect of practical choices of policy which we must make, and make very soon. We have dependencies to deal with and must deal with them in the true spirit of our own institutions. We can give the Filipinos constitutional government, a government which they may count upon to be just, a government based upon some clear and equitable under-standing, intended for their good and not for our aggran-dizement; but we must ourselves for the present supply that government.   It would, it is true, be an unprece-dented operation, reversing the process of Runnymede, but America has before this shown the world enlightened pro-cesses of politics that were without precedent.   It would have been within the choice of John to summon his barons to Runnymede and of his own initiative enter into a con-stitutional understanding with them; and it is within our choice to do a similar thing, at once wise and generous, in the government of the Philippine Islands.   But we cannot give them self-government.   Self-government is not a thing that can be 'given' to any people, because it is a form of character and not a form of constitution.   No people can be 'given' the self-control of maturity.   Only a long appren-ticeship of obedience can secure them the precious pos-session, a thing no more to be bought than given.   They cannot be presented with the character of a community, but it may confidently be hoped that they will become a community under the wholesome and salutary influences of just laws and a sympathetic administration; that they will after a while understand and master themselves, if in the meantime they are understood and served in good con-science by those set over them in authority.

We of all people in the world should know these funda-mental things and should act upon them, if only to illustrate the mastery in politics which belongs to us of hereditary right.   To ignore them would be not only to fail and fail miserably, but to fail ridiculously and belie ourselves. Having ourselves gained self-government by a definite process which can have no substitute, let us put the peo-ples dependent upon us in the right way to gain it also.

# III

IT is difficult to describe any single part of a great governmental system without describing the whole of it. Governments are living things and operate as organic wholes. Moreover, governments have their natural evolution and are one thing in one age, another in another. The makers of the Constitution constructed the federal government upon a theory of checks and balances which was meant to limit the operation of each part and allow to no single part or organ of it a dominating force; but no government can be successfully conducted upon so mechanical a theory. [Leadership and control must be lodged somewhere; the whole art of statesmanship is the art of bringing the several parts of government into effective coöperation for the accomplishment of particular common objects, — and party objects at that.] Our study of each part of our federal system, if we are to discover our real government as it lives, must be made to disclose to us its operative coördination as a whole: its places of leadership, its method of action, how it operates, what checks it, what gives it energy and effect. Governments are what politicians make them, and it is easier to write of the President than of the presidency.

The government of the United States was constructed upon the Whig theory of political dynamics, which was a sort of unconscious copy of the Newtonian theory of

54

the universe. In our own day, whenever we discuss the structure or development of anything, whether in nature or in society, we consciously or unconsciously follow Mr. Darwin; but before Mr. Darwin, they followed Newton. Some single law, like the law of gravitation, swung each system of thought and gave it its principle of unity. Every sun, every planet, every free body in the spaces of the heavens, the world itself, is kept in its place and reined to its course by the attraction of bodies that swing with equal order and precision about it, themselves governed by the nice poise and balance of forces which give the whole system of the universe its symmetry and perfect adjustment. The Whigs had tried to give England a similar constitution. They had had no wish to destroy the throne, no conscious desire to reduce the king to a mere figurehead, but had intended only to surround and offset him with a system of constitutional checks and balances which should regulate his otherwise arbitrary course and make it at least always calculable.

They had made no clear analysis of the matter in their own thoughts; it has not been the habit of English politicians, or indeed of English-speaking politicians on either side of the water, to be clear theorists. It was left to a Frenchman to point out to the Whigs what they had done. They had striven to make Parliament so influential in the making of laws and so authoritative in the criticism of the king's policy that the king could in no matter have his own way without their coöperation and assent, though they left him free, the while, if he chose, to interpose an absolute veto upon the acts of Parliament. They had striven to secure for the courts of law as great an independence as possible, so that they might be neither overawed by parliament nor coerced by the king. In brief, as Montesquieu pointed out to them in his lucid way, they had sought to balance executive, legislature, and judiciary off against one another by a series of checks and counterpoises, which Newton might readily have recognized as suggestive of the mechanism of the heavens.

The makers of our federal Constitution followed the scheme as they found it expounded in Montesquieu, followed it with genuine scientific enthusiasm. The admirable expositions of the *Federalist* read like thoughtful applications of Montesquieu to the political needs and circumstances of America. They are full of the theory of checks and balances. The President is balanced off against Congress, Congress against the President, and each against the courts. Our statesmen of the earlier generations quoted no one so often as Montesquieu, and they quoted him always as a scientific standard in the field of politics. Politics is turned into mechanics under his touch. The theory of gravitation is supreme.

The trouble with the theory is that government is not a machine, but a living thing. It falls, not under the theory of the universe, but under the theory of organic life. It is accountable to Darwin, not to Newton. It is modified by its environment, necessitated by its tasks, shaped to its functions by the sheer pressure of life. No living thing can have its organs offset against each other as checks, and live. On the contrary, its life is dependent upon their quick coöperation, their ready response to the commands of instinct or intelligence, their amicable community of purpose. Government is not a body of blind forces; it is a body of men, with highly differentiated functions, no doubt, in our modern day of specialization, but with a common task and purpose. Their coöperation is indispensable, their warfare fatal. There can be no successful government without leadership or without the intimate, almost instinctive, coördination of the organs of life and action. This is not theory, but fact, and displays its force as fact, whatever theories may be thrown across its track. Living political constitutions must be Darwinian in structure and in practice.

Fortunately, the definitions and prescriptions of our constitutional law, though conceived in the Newtonian spirit and upon the Newtonian principle, are sufficiently broad and elastic to allow for the play of life and circumstance. Though they were Whig theorists, the men who framed the federal Constitution were also practical statesmen with an experienced eye for affairs and a quick practical sagacity in respect of the actual structure of government, and they have given us a thoroughly workable model. If it had in fact been a machine governed by mechanically automatic balances, it would have had no history; but it was not, and its history has been rich with the influences and personalities of the men who have conducted it and made it a living reality. The government of the United States has had a vital and normal organic growth and has proved itself eminently adapted to express the changing temper and purposes of the American people from age to age.

That is the reason why it is easier to write of the President than of the presidency. The presidency has been one thing at one time, another at another, varying with the man who occupied the office and with the circumstances that surrounded him. One account must be given of the office during the period 1789 to 1825, when the government was getting its footing both at home and abroad, struggling for its place among the nations and its full credit among its own people; when English precedents and traditions were strongest; and when the men chosen for the office were men bred to leadership in a way that attracted to them the attention and confidence of the whole country. Another account must be given of it during Jackson's time, when an imperious man, bred not in deliberative assemblies or quiet councils, but in the field and upon a rough frontier, worked his own will upon affairs, with or without formal sanction of law, sustained by a clear undoubting conscience and the love of a people who had grown deeply impatient of the régime he had supplanted. Still another account must be given of it during the years 1836 to 1861, when domestic affairs of many debatable kinds absorbed the country, when Congress necessarily exercised the chief choices of policy, and when the Presidents who followed one another in office lacked the personal force and initiative to make for themselves a leading place in counsel. After that came the Civil War and Mr. Lincoln's unique task and achievement, when the executive seemed for a little while to become by sheer stress of circumstances the whole government, Congress merely voting supplies and assenting to necessary laws, as Parliament did in the time of the Tudors. From 1865 to 1898 domestic questions, legislative matters in respect of which Congress had naturally to make the initial choice, legislative leaders the chief decisions of policy, came once more to the front, and no President except Mr. Cleveland played a leading and decisive part in the quiet drama of our national life. Even Mr. Cleveland may be said to have owed his great rôle in affairs rather to his own native force and the confused politics of the time, than to any opportunity of leadership naturally afforded him by a system which had subordinated so many Presidents before him to Congress. The war with Spain again changed the balance of parts. Foreign questions became leading questions again, as they had been in the first days of the government, and in them the President was of necessity leader. Our new place in the affairs of the world has since that year of transformation kept him at the front of our government, where our own thoughts and the attention of men everywhere is centred upon him.

Both men and circumstances have created these contrasts in the administration and influence of the office of President. We have all been disciples of Montesquieu, but we have also been practical politicians. Mr. Bagehot once remarked that it was no proof of the excellence of the Constitution of the United States that the Americans had operated it with conspicuous success because the Americans could run any constitution successfully; and, while the compliment is altogether acceptable, it is certainly true that our practical sense is more noticeable than our theoretical consistency, and that, while we were once all constitutional lawyers, we are in these latter days apt to be very impatient of literal and dogmatic interpretations of constitutional principle.

The makers of the Constitution seem to have thought of the President as what the stricter Whig theorists wished the king to be: only the legal executive, the presiding and guiding authority in the application of law and the execution of policy. His veto upon legislation was only his 'check' on Congress, — was a power of restraint, not of guidance. He was empowered to prevent bad laws, but he was not to be given an opportunity to make good ones. As a matter of fact he has become very much more. He has become the leader of his party and the guide of the nation in political purpose, and therefore in legal action. The constitutional structure of the government has hampered and limited his action in these significant rôles, but it has not prevented it. The influence of the President has varied with the men who have been Presidents and with the circumstances of their times, but the tendency has been unmistakably disclosed, and springs out of the very nature of government itself. It is merely the proof that our government is a living, organic thing, and must, like every other government, work out the close synthesis of active parts which can exist only when leadership is lodged in some one man or group of men. You cannot compound a successful government out of antagonisms. Greatly as the practice and influence of Presidents has varied, there can be no mistaking the fact that we have grown more and more inclined from generation to generation to look to the President as the unifying force in our complex system, the leader both of his party and of the nation. To do so is not inconsistent with the actual provisions of the Constitution; it is only inconsistent with a very mechanical theory of its meaning and intention. The Constitution contains no theories. It is as practical a document as Magna Carta.

The rôle of party leader is forced upon the President by the method of his selection. The theory of the makers of the Constitution may have been that the presidential electors would exercise a real choice, but it is hard to understand how, as experienced politicians, they can have expected anything of the kind. They did not provide that

the electors should meet as one body for consultation and
make deliberate choice of a President and Vice-President,
but that they should meet "in their respective states"
and cast their ballots in separate groups, without the
possibility of consulting and without the least likelihood
of agreeing, unless some such means as have actually been
used were employed to suggest and determine their choice
beforehand.    It was the practice at first to make party
nominations for the presidency by congressional caucus.
Since the Democratic upheaval of General Jackson's time
nominating conventions have taken the place of congressional caucuses; and the choice of Presidents by party
conventions has had some very interesting results.

We are apt to think of the choice of nominating conventions as somewhat haphazard.    We know, or think that
we know, how their action is sometimes determined, and
the knowledge makes us very uneasy.    We know that
there is no debate in nominating conventions, no discussion
of the merits of the respective candidates, at which the
country can sit as audience and assess the wisdom of the
final choice.    If there is any talking to be done, aside
from the formal addresses of the temporary and permanent
chairmen and of those who present the platform and the
names of the several aspirants for nomination, the assembly
adjourns.    The talking that is to decide the result must be
done in private committee rooms and behind the closed
doors of the headquarters of the several state delegations
to the convention.    The intervals between sessions are
filled with a very feverish activity.    Messengers run from
one headquarters to another until the small hours of the
morning.    Conference follows conference in a way that
is likely to bring newspaper correspondents to the verge

of despair, it being next to impossible to put the rumors together into any coherent story of what is going on. Only at the rooms of the national committee of the party is there any clear knowledge of the situation as a whole; and the excitement of the members of the convention rises from session to session under the sheer pressure of uncertainty. The final majority is compounded no outsider and few members can tell how.

Many influences, too, play upon nominating conventions, which seem mere winds of feeling. They sit in great halls, with galleries into which crowd thousands of spectators from all parts of the country, but chiefly, of course, from the place at which the convention sits, and the feeling of the galleries is transmitted to the floor. The cheers of mere spectators echo the names of popular candidates, and every excitement on the floor is enhanced a hundred fold in the galleries. Sudden gusts of impulse are apt to change the whole feeling of the convention, and offset in a moment the most careful arrangements of managing politicians. It has come to be a commonly accepted opinion that if the Republican convention of 1860 had not met in Chicago, it would have nominated Mr. Seward and not Mr. Lincoln. Mr. Seward was the acknowledged leader of the new party; had been its most telling spokesman; had given its tenets definition and currency. Mr. Lincoln had not been brought within view of the country as a whole until the other day, when he had given Mr. Douglas so hard a fight to keep his seat in the Senate, and had but just now given currency among thoughtful men to the striking phrases of the searching speeches he had made in debate with his practised antagonist. But the convention met in Illinois, amidst throngs of Mr. Lincoln's ardent friends and advocates. His managers saw to it that the galleries were properly filled with men who would cheer every mention of his name until the hall was shaken. Every influence of the place worked for him and he was chosen.

Thoughtful critics of our political practices have not allowed the excellence of the choice to blind them to the danger of the method. They have known too many examples of what the galleries have done to supplement the efforts of managing politicians to feel safe in the presence of processes which seem rather those of intrigue and impulse than those of sober choice. They can cite instances, moreover, of sudden, unlooked-for excitements on the floor of such bodies which have swept them from the control of all sober influences and hastened them to choices which no truly deliberative assembly could ever have made. There is no training school for Presidents, unless, as some governors have wished, it be looked for in the governorships of states; and nominating conventions have confined themselves in their selections to no class, have demanded of aspirants no particular experience or knowledge of affairs. They have nominated lawyers without political experience, soldiers, editors of newspapers, newspaper correspondents, whom they pleased, without regard to their lack of contact with affairs. It would seem as if their choices were almost matters of chance.

In reality there is much more method, much more definite purpose, much more deliberate choice in the extraordinary process than there seems to be. The leading spirits of the national committee of each party could give an account of the matter which would put a very different face on it and make the methods of nominating conventions seem, for all the undoubted elements of chance there are in them, on the whole very manageable. Moreover, the party that expects to win may be counted on to make a much more conservative and thoughtful selection of a candidate than the party that merely hopes to win. The haphazard selections which seem to discredit the system are generally made by conventions of the party unaccustomed to success. Success brings sober calculation and a sense of responsibility.

And it must be remembered also that our political system is not so coördinated as to supply a training for presidential aspirants or even to make it absolutely necessary that they should have had extended experience in public affairs. Certainly the country has never thought of members of Congress as in any particular degree fitted for the presidency. Even the Vice President is not afforded an opportunity to learn the duties of the office. The men best prepared, no doubt, are those who have been governors of states or members of cabinets. And yet even they are chosen for their respective offices generally by reason of a kind of fitness and availability which does not necessarily argue in them the size and power that would fit them for the greater office. In our earlier practice cabinet officers were regarded as in the natural line of succession to the presidency. Mr. Jefferson had been in General Washington's cabinet, Mr. Madison in Mr. Jefferson's, Mr. Monroe in Mr. Madison's; and generally it was the Secretary of State who was taken. But those were days when English precedent was strong upon us, when cabinets were expected to be made up of the political leaders of the party in power; and from their ranks subsequent candidates for the presidency were most likely to be selected. The practice, as we look back to it, seems eminently sensible, and we wonder why it should have been so soon departed from and apparently forgotten. We wonder, too, why eminent senators have not sometimes been chosen; why members of the House have so seldom commanded the attention of nominating conventions; why public life has never offered itself in any definite way as a preparation for the presidential office.

If the matter be looked at a little more closely, it will be seen that the office of President, as we have used and developed it, really does not demand actual experience in affairs so much as particular qualities of mind and character which we are at least as likely to find outside the ranks of our public men as within them. What is it that a nominating convention wants in the man it is to present to the country for its suffrages? A man who will be and who will seem to the country in some sort an embodiment of the character and purpose it wishes its government to have, — a man who understands his own day and the needs of the country, and who has the personality and the initiative to enforce his views both upon the people and upon Congress. It may seem an odd way to get such a man. It is even possible that nominating conventions and those who guide them do not realize entirely what it is that they do. But in simple fact the convention picks out a party leader from the body of the nation. Not that it expects its nominee to direct the interior government of the party and to supplant its already accredited and experienced spokesmen in Congress and in its state and national committees; but it does of necessity expect him to represent it before public opinion and to stand before the country as its representative man, as a true type of what the country may

F

expect of the party itself in purpose and principle. It cannot but be led by him in the campaign; if he be elected, it cannot but acquiesce in his leadership of the government itself. What the country will demand of the candidate will be, not that he be an astute politician, skilled and practised in affairs, but that he be a man such as it can trust, in character, in intention, in knowledge of its needs, in perception of the best means by which those needs may be met, in capacity to prevail by reason of his own weight and integrity. Sometimes the country believes in a party, but more often it believes in a man; and conventions have often shown the instinct to perceive which it is that the country needs in a particular presidential year, a mere representative partisan, a military hero, or some one who will genuinely speak for the country itself, whatever be his training and antecedents. It is in this sense that the President has the rôle of party leader thrust upon him by the very method by which he is chosen.

As legal executive, his constitutional aspect, the President cannot be thought of alone. He cannot execute laws. Their actual daily execution must be taken care of by the several executive departments and by the now innumerable body of federal officials throughout the country. In respect of the strictly executive duties of his office the President may be said to administer the presidency in conjunction with the members of his cabinet, like the chairman of a commission. He is even of necessity much less active in the actual carrying out of the law than are his colleagues and advisers. It is therefore becoming more and more true, as the business of the government becomes more and more complex and extended, that the President is becoming more and more a political and less and less an executive officer. His executive powers are in commission, while his political powers more and more centre and accumulate upon him and are in their very nature personal and inalienable.

Only the larger sort of executive questions are brought to him. Departments which run with easy routine and whose transactions bring few questions of general policy to the surface may proceed with their business for months and even years together without demanding his attention; and no department is in any sense under his direct charge. Cabinet meetings do not discuss detail: they are concerned only with the larger matters of policy or expediency which important business is constantly disclosing. There are no more hours in the President's day than in another man's. If he is indeed the executive, he must act almost entirely by delegation, and is in the hands of his colleagues. He is likely to be praised if things go well, and blamed if they go wrong; but his only real control is of the persons to whom he deputes the performance of executive duties. It is through no fault or neglect of his that the duties apparently assigned to him by the Constitution have come to be his less conspicuous, less important duties, and that duties apparently not assigned to him at all chiefly occupy his time and energy. The one set of duties it has proved practically impossible for him to perform; the other it has proved impossible for him to escape.

He cannot escape being the leader of his party except by incapacity and lack of personal force, because he is at once the choice of the party and of the nation. He is the party nominee, and the only party nominee for whom the whole nation votes. Members of the House and Senate are representatives of localities, are voted for only by sections of voters, or by local bodies of electors like the members of the state legislatures. There is no national party choice except that of President. No one else represents the people as a whole, exercising a national choice; and inasmuch as his strictly executive duties are in fact subordinated, so far at any rate as all detail is concerned, the President represents not so much the party's governing efficiency as its controlling ideals and principles. He is not so much part of its organization as its vital link of connection with the thinking nation. He can dominate his party by being spokesman for the real sentiment and purpose of the country, by giving direction to opinion, by giving the country at once the information and the statements of policy which will enable it to form its judgments alike of parties and of men.

For he is also the political leader of the nation, or has it in his choice to be. The nation as a whole has chosen him, and is conscious that it has no other political spokesman. His is the only national voice in affairs. Let him once win the admiration and confidence of the country, and no other single force can withstand him, no combination of forces will easily overpower him. His position takes the imagination of the country. He is the representative of no constituency, but of the whole people. When he speaks in his true character, he speaks for no special interest. If he rightly interpret the national thought and boldly insist upon it, he is irresistible; and the country never feels the zest of action so much as when its President is of such insight and calibre. Its instinct is for unified action, and it craves a single leader. It is for this reason that it will often prefer to choose a man rather than a party. A President whom it trusts can not only lead it, but form it to his own views.

It is the extraordinary isolation imposed upon the President by our system that makes the character and opportunity of his office so extraordinary. In him are centred both opinion and party. He may stand, if he will, a little outside party and insist as if it were upon the general opinion. It is with the instinctive feeling that it is upon occasion such a man that the country wants that nominating conventions will often nominate men who are not their acknowledged leaders, but only such men as the country would like to see lead both its parties. The President may also, if he will, stand within the party counsels and use the advantage of his power and personal force to control its actual programs. He may be both the leader of his party and the leader of the nation, or he may be one or the other. If he lead the nation, his party can hardly resist him. His office is anything he has the sagacity and force to make it.

That is the reason why it has been one thing at one time, another at another. The Presidents who have not made themselves leaders have lived no more truly on that account in the spirit of the Constitution than those whose force has told in the determination of law and policy. No doubt Andrew Jackson overstepped the bounds meant to be set to the authority of his office. It was certainly in direct contravention of the spirit of the Constitution that he should have refused to respect and execute decisions of the Supreme Court of the United States, and no serious student of our history can righteously condone what he did in such matters on the ground that his intentions were upright and his principles pure. But the Constitution of the United States is not a mere lawyers' document: it is a vehicle of life, and its spirit is always the spirit of the age. Its prescriptions are clear and we know what they are; a written document makes lawyers of us all, and our duty as citizens should make us conscientious lawyers, reading the text of the Constitution without subtlety or sophistication; but life is always your last and most authoritative critic.

Some of our Presidents have deliberately held themselves off from using the full power they might legitimately have used, because of conscientious scruples, because they were more theorists than statesmen. They have held the strict literary theory of the Constitution, the Whig theory, the Newtonian theory, and have acted as if they thought that Pennsylvania Avenue should have been even longer than it is; that there should be no intimate communication of any kind between the Capitol and the White House; that the President as a man was no more at liberty to lead the houses of Congress by persuasion than he was at liberty as President to dominate them by authority, — supposing that he had, what he has not, authority enough to dominate them. But the makers of the Constitution were not enacting Whig theory, they were not making laws with the expectation that, not the laws themselves, but their opinions, known by future historians to lie back of them, should govern the constitutional action of the country. They were statesmen, not pedants, and their laws are sufficient to keep us to the paths they set us upon. The President is at liberty, both in law and conscience, to be as big a man as he can. His capacity will set the limit; and if Congress be overborne by him, it will be no fault of the makers of the Constitution, — it will be from no lack of constitutional powers on its part, but only because the President has the nation behind him, and Congress has not.

He has no means of compelling Congress except through public opinion.

That I say he has no means of compelling Congress will show what I mean, and that my meaning has no touch of radicalism or iconoclasm in it.   There are illegitimate means by which the President may influence the action of Congress. He may bargain with members, not only with regard to appointments, but also with regard to legislative measures. He may use his local patronage to assist members to get or retain their seats.   He may interpose his powerful influence, in one covert way or another, in contests for places in the Senate.   He may also overbear Congress by arbitrary acts which ignore the laws or virtually override them. He may even substitute his own orders for acts of Congress which he wants but cannot get.   Such things are not only deeply immoral, they are destructive of the fundamental understandings of constitutional government and, therefore, of constitutional government itself.   They are sure, moreover, in a country of free public opinion, to bring their own punishment, to destroy both the fame and the power of the man who dares to practise them.   No honorable man includes such agencies in a sober exposition of the Constitution or allows himself to think of them when he speaks of the influences of "life" which govern each generation's use and interpretation of that great instrument, our sovereign guide and the object of our deepest reverence. Nothing in a system like ours can be constitutional which is immoral or which touches the good faith of those who have sworn to obey the fundamental law.   The reprobation of all good men will always overwhelm such influences with shame and failure.   But the personal force of the President is perfectly constitutional to any extent to which he chooses to exercise it, and it is by the clear logic of our constitutional practice that he has become alike the leader of his party and the leader of the nation.

The political powers of the President are not quite so obvious in their scope and character when we consider his relations with Congress as when we consider his relations to his party and to the nation. They need, therefore, a somewhat more critical examination. Leadership in government naturally belongs to its executive officers, who are daily in contact with practical conditions and exigencies and whose reputations alike for good judgment and for fidelity are at stake much more than are those of the members of the legislative body at every turn of the law's application. The law-making part of the government ought certainly to be very hospitable to the suggestions of the planning and acting part of it. Those Presidents who have felt themselves bound to adhere to the strict literary theory of the Constitution have scrupulously refrained from attempting to determine either the subjects or the character of legislation, except so far as they were obliged to decide for themselves, after Congress had acted, whether they should acquiesce in it or not. And yet the Constitution explicitly authorizes the President to recommend to Congress "such measures as he shall deem necessary and expedient," and it is not necessary to the integrity of even the literary theory of the Constitution to insist that such recommendations should be merely perfunctory. Certainly General Washington did not so regard them, and he stood much nearer the Whig theory than we do. A President's messages to Congress have no more weight or authority than their intrinsic reasonableness and importance give them: but that is their only constitutional

limitation.  The Constitution certainly does not forbid the
President to back them up, as General Washington did,
with such personal force and influence as he may possess.
Some of our Presidents have felt the need, which unquestionably exists in our system, for some spokesman of
the nation as a whole, in matters of legislation no less than
in other matters, and have tried to supply Congress with
the leadership of suggestion, backed by argument and by
iteration and by every legitimate appeal to public opinion.
Cabinet officers are shut out from Congress; the President
himself has, by custom, no access to its floor; many long-
established barriers of precedent, though not of law,
hinder him from exercising any direct influence upon its
deliberations; and yet he is undoubtedly the only spokesman of the whole people.  They have again and again, as
often as they were afforded the opportunity, manifested
their satisfaction when he has boldly accepted the rôle
of leader, to which the peculiar origin and character of his
authority entitle him.  The Constitution bids him speak,
and times of stress and change must more and more thrust
upon him the attitude of originator of policies.

His is the vital place of action in the system, whether he
accept it as such or not, and the office is the measure of the
man, — of his wisdom as well as of his force.  His veto
abundantly equips him to stay the hand of Congress when
he will.  It is seldom possible to pass a measure over his
veto, and no President has hesitated to use the veto when
his own judgment of the public good was seriously at issue
with that of the houses.  The veto has never been suffered
to fall into even temporary disuse with us.  In England it
has ceased to exist, with the change in the character of the
executive.  There has been no veto since Anne's day,

because ever since the reign of Anne the laws of England have been originated either by ministers who spoke the king's own will or by ministers whom the king did not dare gainsay; and in our own time the ministers who formulate the laws are themselves the executive of the nation; a veto would be a negative upon their own power. If bills pass of which they disapprove, they resign and give place to the leaders of those who approve them. The framers of the Constitution made in our President a more powerful, because a more isolated, king than the one they were imitating; and because the Constitution gave them their veto in such explicit terms, our Presidents have not hesitated to use it, even when it put their mere individual judgment against that of large majorities in both houses of Congress. And yet in the exercise of the power to suggest legislation, quite as explicitly conferred upon them by the Constitution, some of our Presidents have seemed to have a timid fear that they might offend some law of taste which had become a constitutional principle.

In one sense their messages to Congress have no more authority than the letters of any other citizen would have. Congress can heed or ignore them as it pleases; and there have been periods of our history when presidential messages were utterly without practical significance, perfunctory documents which few persons except the editors of newspapers took the trouble to read. But if the President has personal force and cares to exercise it, there is this tremendous difference between his messages and the views of any other citizen, either outside Congress or in it: that the whole country reads them and feels that the writer speaks with an authority and a responsibility which the people themselves have given him.

The history of our cabinets affords a striking illustration of the progress of the idea that the President is not merely the legal head but also the political leader of the nation. In the earlier days of the government it was customary for the President to fill his cabinet with the recognized leaders of his party. General Washington even tried the experiment which William of Orange tried at the very beginning of the era of cabinet government. He called to his aid the leaders of both political parties, associating Mr. Hamilton with Mr. Jefferson, on the theory that all views must be heard and considered in the conduct of the government. That was the day in which English precedent prevailed, and English cabinets were made up of the chief political characters of the day. But later years have witnessed a marked change in our practice, in this as in many other things. The old tradition was indeed slow in dying out. It persisted with considerable vitality at least until General Garfield's day, and may yet from time to time revive, for many functions of our cabinets justify it and make it desirable. But our later Presidents have apparently ceased to regard the cabinet as a council of party leaders such as the party they represent would have chosen. They look upon it rather as a body of personal advisers whom the President chooses from the ranks of those whom he personally trusts and prefers to look to for advice. Our recent Presidents have not sought their associates among those whom the fortunes of party contest have brought into prominence and influence, but have called their personal friends and business colleagues to cabinet positions, and men who have given proof of their efficiency in private, not in public, life, — bankers who had never had any place in the formal counsels of the party, eminent lawyers who had held aloof from politics, private secretaries who had shown an unusual sagacity and proficiency in handling public business; as if the President were himself alone the leader of his party, the members of his cabinet only his private advisers, at any rate advisers of his private choice. Mr. Cleveland may be said to have been the first President to make this conception of the cabinet prominent in his choices, and he did not do so until his second administration. Mr. Roosevelt has emphasized the idea.

Upon analysis it seems to mean this: the cabinet is an executive, not a political body. The President cannot himself be the actual executive; he must therefore find, to act in his stead, men of the best legal and business gifts, and depend upon them for the actual administration of the government in all its daily activities. If he seeks political advice of his executive colleagues, he seeks it because he relies upon their natural good sense and experienced judgment, upon their knowledge of the country and its business and social conditions, upon their sagacity as representative citizens of more than usual observation and discretion; not because they are supposed to have had any very intimate contact with politics or to have made a profession of public affairs. He has chosen, not representative politicians, but eminent representative citizens, selecting them rather for their special fitness for the great business posts to which he has assigned them than for their political experience, and looking to them for advice in the actual conduct of the government rather than in the shaping of political policy. They are, in his view, not necessarily political officers at all.

It may with a great deal of plausibility be argued that the Constitution looks upon the President himself in the same way. It does not seem to make him a prime minister or the leader of the nation's counsels. Some Presidents are, therefore, and some are not. It depends upon the man and his gifts. He may be like his cabinet, or he may be more than his cabinet. His office is a mere vantage ground from which he may be sure that effective words of advice and timely efforts at reform will gain telling momentum. He has the ear of the nation as of course, and a great person may use such an advantage greatly. If he use the opportunity, he may take his cabinet into partnership or not, as he pleases; and so its character may vary with his. Self-reliant men will regard their cabinets as executive councils; men less self-reliant or more prudent will regard them as also political councils, and will wish to call into them men who have earned the confidence of their party. The character of the cabinet may be made a nice index of the theory of the presidential office, as well as of the President's theory of party government; but the one view is, so far as I can see, as constitutional as the other.

One of the greatest of the President's powers I have not yet spoken of at all: his control, which is very absolute, of the foreign relations of the nation. The initiative in foreign affairs, which the President possesses without any restriction whatever, is virtually the power to control them absolutely. The President cannot conclude a treaty with a foreign power without the consent of the Senate, but he may guide every step of diplomacy, and to guide diplomacy is to determine what treaties must be made, if the faith and prestige of the government are to be maintained. He need disclose no step of negotiation until it is complete, and when in any critical matter it is completed the government is virtually committed.  Whatever its disinclination, the Senate may feel itself committed also.

I have not dwelt upon this power of the President, because it has been decisively influential in determining the character and influence of the office at only two periods in our history; at the very first, when the government was young and had so to use its incipient force as to win the respect of the nations into whose family it had thrust itself, and in our own day when the results of the Spanish War, the ownership of distant possessions, and many sharp struggles for foreign trade make it necessary that we should turn our best talents to the task of dealing firmly, wisely, and justly with political and commercial rivals. The President can never again be the mere domestic figure he has been throughout so large a part of our history.  The nation has risen to the first rank in power and resources.  The other nations of the world look askance upon her, half in envy, half in fear, and wonder with a deep anxiety what she will do with her vast strength.  They receive the frank professions of men like Mr. John Hay, whom we wholly trusted, with a grain of salt, and doubt what we were sure of, their truthfulness and sincerity, suspecting a hidden design under every utterance he makes.  Our President must always, henceforth, be one of the great powers of the world, whether he act greatly and wisely or not, and the best statesmen we can produce will be needed to fill the office of Secretary of State.  We have but begun to see the presidential office in this light; but it is the light which will more and more beat upon it, and more and more determine its character and its effect upon the politics of the nation.  We can never hide our President again as a mere domestic officer.

We can never again see him the mere executive he was in the thirties and forties.  He must stand always at the front of our affairs, and the office will be as big and as influential as the man who occupies it.

How is it possible to sum up the duties and influence of such an office in such a system in comprehensive terms which will cover all its changeful aspects?  In the view of the makers of the Constitution the President was to be legal executive; perhaps the leader of the nation; certainly not the leader of the party, at any rate while in office.  But by the operation of forces inherent in the very nature of government he has become all three, and by inevitable consequence the most heavily burdened officer in the world. No other man's day is so full as his, so full of the responsibilities which tax mind and conscience alike and demand an inexhaustible vitality.  The mere task of making appointments to office, which the Constitution imposes upon the President, has come near to breaking some of our Presidents down, because it is a never-ending task in a civil service not yet put upon a professional footing, confused with short terms of office, always forming and dissolving. And in proportion as the President ventures to use his opportunity to lead opinion and act as spokesman of the people in affairs the people stand ready to overwhelm him by running to him with every question, great and small. They are as eager to have him settle a literary question as a political; hear him as acquiescently with regard to matters of special expert knowledge as with regard to public affairs, and call upon him to quiet all troubles by his personal intervention.  Men of ordinary physique and discretion cannot be Presidents and live, if the strain be not somehow relieved.  We shall be obliged always to be picking our chief magistrates from among wise and prudent athletes, — a small class.

The future development of the presidency, therefore, must certainly, one would confidently predict, run along such lines as the President's later relations with his cabinet suggest. General Washington, partly out of unaffected modesty, no doubt, but also out of the sure practical instinct which he possessed in so unusual a degree, set an example which few of his successors seem to have followed in any systematic manner. He made constant and intimate use of his colleagues in every matter that he handled, seeking their assistance and advice by letter when they were at a distance and he could not obtain it in person. It is well known to all close students of our history that his greater state papers, even those which seem in some peculiar and intimate sense his personal utterances, are full of the ideas and the very phrases of the men about him whom he most trusted. His rough drafts came back to him from Mr. Hamilton and Mr. Madison in great part rephrased and rewritten, in many passages reconceived and given a new color. He thought and acted always by the light of counsel, with a will and definite choice of his own, but through the instrumentality of other minds as well as his own. The duties and responsibilities laid upon the President by the Constitution can be changed only by constitutional amendment, — a thing too difficult to attempt except upon some greater necessity than the relief of an overburdened office, even though that office be the greatest in the land; and it is to be doubted whether the deliberate opinion of the country would consent to make of the President a less powerful officer than he is. He can secure his own relief without shirking any real responsibility. Appoint-

ments, for example, he can, if he will, make more and more
upon the advice and choice of his executive colleagues;
every matter of detail not only, but also every minor matter
of counsel or of general policy, he can more and more
depend upon his chosen advisers to determine; he need
reserve for himself only the larger matters of counsel and
that general oversight of the business of the government
and of the persons who conduct it which is not possible
without intimate daily consultations, indeed, but which
is possible without attempting the intolerable burden of
direct control. This is, no doubt, the idea of their functions
which most Presidents have entertained and which most
Presidents suppose themselves to have acted on; but we
have reason to believe that most of our Presidents have
taken their duties too literally and have attempted the
impossible. But we can safely predict that as the multitude of the President's duties increases, as it must with
the growth and widening activities of the nation itself, the
incumbents of the great office will more and more come to
feel that they are administering it in its truest purpose
and with greatest effect by regarding themselves as less
and less executive officers and more and more directors of
affairs and leaders of the nation, — men of counsel and of
the sort of action that makes for enlightenment.

## IV

## THE HOUSE OF REPRESENTATIVES

THE President of the United States was intended by the makers of the Constitution to be a reformed and standardized king, after the Whig model; and Congress was meant to be a reformed and properly regulated parliament. But both President and Congress have broken from the mold and adapted themselves to circumstances, after a thoroughly American fashion, — partly because the king and Parliament which the convention of 1787 intended to copy, with modifications, had no real existence and were therefore largely theoretical, but chiefly because, even if they had existed at the moment the copy was made, they could not have been fixed in that transitional form by any law that the convention could have devised. They were sure to undergo rapid alteration in one direction or another, and each has taken its own course of change. It would be difficult now to believe that the American President and the English King, the American Congress and the English Parliament, were originally of the same model and intention if we did not clearly recollect the fact to be so.

It is the reaction of the several parts of government upon one another that gives each part its final form and character. It is useless to study any living structure of government anatomically, in its separate parts. Its character and significance come to light, as I have already several times insisted, only when we study it as an organic whole, living and acting from day to day. Our present study must at every stage be a study of the synthesis of power in the government on the one hand, and of the people's control of the government on the other; for there can be no power which is not synthetic, which does not operate with organic unity; and there can be no constitutional government where the organs of government are not constantly under the control of public opinion. We shall get our completest understanding of the House of Representatives, therefore, if we look at it from two points of view: from the point of view of its synthesis with the other parts of the Government, and from the point of view of its relations to opinion.

If you were to ask an Englishman to describe the government of England, he would of course include the Parliament in his description. Indeed, it is likely that he would have more to say of the House of Commons than of anything else. But if you were to speak to him of 'The Government,' he would not think of the House of Commons but only of the ministers, of what we should call the administration. I can make the part played by the House of Representatives in our system clearest by contrasting it with the English House of Commons, and in order to make that contrast carry its full significance it is necessary that we should bear these two meanings of the word government in mind and never confuse them. When I said in a previous lecture that it was not necessary for the full realization of constitutional government that representative assemblies should become a part of the 'Government,' I meant, of course, a part of the administrative organ of government, the organ that is looked to for initiative, which makes choice of policy and actually controls the life of the nation under the laws ; and the significant difference between English and American political development is that in America Congress has become part of the Government, while in England Parliament has not.  Parliament is still, as it was originally intended to be, the grand assize, or session, of the nation, to criticize and control the Government.  It is not a council to administer it.  It does not originate its own bills, except in minor matters which seem to spring out of public opinion or out of the special circumstances of particular interests, rather than out of the conduct of government.  Every legislative proposition of capital importance comes to it from the ministers.  The duties of the ministers are not merely executive: the ministers are the Government.  They look to Parliament, not for commands what to do, but for support in their own programs, whether of legal change or of political policy.

What the House of Commons does, therefore, is not to act in any strictly originative way as the law-making body of the nation, but to make and unmake Governments, to prefer now one, and again another, committee of its leading members as its guides, not itself leading but choosing how it shall be led, insisting that the king make the leaders of its own choice the ministers of the crown.  It is not the Government, but its leaders are.  In the supreme act of insisting that they and no others shall be chosen by the crown for the executive posts of government it exhausts its originative force.  Thereafter it follows and criticizes as of old.

Our Congress, on the contrary, does not make or unmake our Government.  The people do that in their selection of a President.  And because Congress cannot make or unmake the Government at its pleasure, it usually makes it a point of pride not to be led by the Government in what it regards as its proper and exclusive sphere, the making of laws.] The making of laws is a very practical matter. It is not a mere enactment of opinions into commands. At least, it should not be. Neither should it be a means of forcing the favorite reforms of some members of the legislative body upon the nation, unless there is to be some direct and easy way of holding those members responsible for the untoward results of their intended reforms, should they fail to bring about the happy changes they were meant to effect. The practical side of law is its application. The Government, therefore, is the only possible body of experts with regard to the practicability and necessity of alterations in the law, and it is certainly a noteworthy outcome of our political development that the houses should have rejected the leadership of the Government in legislation. They stand alone among the legislatures of the world in having done so. It is in this sense that I speak when I say that the American Congress has become a part of the Government, and that the English Parliament never has. [Our Congress freely and habitually originates law upon every subject upon its own initiative, plays a planning and devising part in the conduct of government, and is in many ways an administrative council acting in complete independence of those who are charged with actual administration.] It even resents suggestions from administrative officers as impertinent invasions of its independence. It has in a thousand particulars taken charge of the Government, without assuming the responsibility of putting its leaders in to conduct it. A sharper contrast to the development of the English House of Commons, upon which it was modeled, could hardly be

imagined.   The House of Representatives has moved to
the opposite pole both of theory and of action.

The Senate was, no doubt, meant to be a part of the
Government.   In the making of treaties with foreign
governments and in the difficult and responsible business
of appointments to office it was deliberately associated
with the President as an administrative council, by the
terms of the Constitution.   But these are matters of consultation, in which it waits upon the executive.   The
Senate was not given the initiative in respect of them.   It
cannot originate treaties or make, or even suggest, appointments.   It waits upon the initiative of the Government,
as Parliament does, and has not departed from the original
model.   But in legislative matters proper its attitude is
the same as the attitude of the House.   House and Senate
alike jealously guard their right to be their own guides in
legislation, even when the laws they handle are clearly
administrative in character and deal not with general
matters but with the duties of the executive departments
and the details of governmental business.

The development of our Congress thus affords a singular
and instructive contradiction between theory and fact,
which ought to interest practical politicians as much as
it naturally interests historians.   Congress and Parliament
had the same origin.   Our houses were conceived by the
makers of the Constitution at a period when both Parliament and Congress were supposed to stand outside Government, its mentors and critics, holding aloof from it and
yet determining its action, at any rate negatively, by
what they consented to make legal or insisted upon making
illegal.   And yet our houses, developed under a theory of
checks and balances which seemed intended to preserve that

theory of separateness, have thrust themselves into the business of governing; while Parliament, frankly developed in these later years upon the theory of drawing the several parts of government together in close synthesis, has remained separate and still waits upon the Government for action.

By natural consequence, the organization of our legislative houses is entirely unlike that of Parliament. Having made up their minds to be indeed separate from the executive, to have a distinct life and an independent initiative, and to make themselves part of the Government upon a plan of their own, they have been obliged to create a suitable organization. The House of Representatives, being the more numerous body and in the nature of the case harder to organize as an originative and independent assembly, has effected the more thorough organization, and devotes itself to business with a precision and ease of method which the Senate has not attempted.

The House and Senate are naturally unlike. They are different both in constitution and character. They do not represent the same things. [The House of Representatives is by intention the popular chamber, meant to represent the people by direct election through an extensive suffrage, while the Senate was designed to represent the states as political units, as the constituent members of the Union.] The terms of membership in the two houses, moreover, are different. The two chambers were unquestionably intended to derive their authority from different sources and to speak with different voices in affairs; and however much they may have departed from their original characters in the changeful processes of our politics, they still present many sharp contrasts to one another, and must be described as playing, not the same, but very distinct and dissimilar rôles in affairs.

Perhaps the contrast between them is in certain respects even sharper and clearer now than in the earlier days of our history, when the House was smaller and its functions simpler. The House once debated; now it does not debate. It has not the time. There would be too many debaters, and there are too many subjects of debate. It is a business body, and it must get its business done. When the late Mr. Reed once, upon a well-known occasion, thanked God that the House was not a deliberate assembly, there was no doubt a dash of half-cynical humor in the remark, such as so often gave spice and biting force to what he said, but there was the sober earnest of a serious man of affairs, too. He knew the vast mass of business the House undertook to transact: that it had made itself a great organ of direction, and that it would be impossible for it to get through its calendars if it were to attempt to discuss in open house, instead of in its committee rooms, the measures it acted upon. The Senate has retained its early rules of procedure without material alteration. It is still a place of free and prolonged debate. It will not curtail the privilege of its members to say what they please, at whatever length. But the senators are comparatively few in number; they can afford the indulgence. The House cannot. The Senate may remain individualistic, atomistic, but the House must be organic, — an efficient instrument, not a talkative assembly.

A numerous body like the House of Representatives is naturally and of course unfit for organic, creative action through debate. Debate, indeed, is not a creative process. It is critical. It does not produce; it tests. A large assembly cannot form policies or formulate measures, and the House of Representatives is merely a large assembly, like any other public meeting in its unfitness for business. Like other public meetings, it must send committees out to formulate its resolves. It organizes itself, therefore, into committees, — not occasional committees, formed from time to time, but standing committees permanently charged with its business and given every prerogative of suggestion and explanation, in order that each piece of legislative business may be systematically attended to by a body small enough to digest and perfect it.

For each important subject of legislation there is a standing committee. There is, for example, a Committee on Appropriations, a Committee on Ways and Means, that is, on the sources and objects of taxation, a Committee on Banking and Currency, a Committee on Commerce, a Committee on Manufactures, a Committee on Agriculture, a Committee on Railways and Canals, a Committee on Rivers and Harbors, a Committee on the Merchant Marine and Fisheries, a Committee on the Judiciary, a Committee on Foreign Affairs, a Committee on Public Lands, a Committee on Land Claims, a Committee on War Claims, a Committee on Post Offices and Post Roads, a Committee on Military Affairs, a Committee on Naval Affairs, a Committee on Indian Affairs, a Committee on Education, a Committee on Labor, — the business likely to be brought to the attention of the House being thoroughly, indeed somewhat minutely, classified and the committees being some fifty-seven in number.

Every bill introduced must be sent to a committee. It would probably be impossible to think of any legitimate subject for legislation upon which a bill could be drawn up for whose consideration no standing committee has been provided. If a new subject should turn up, the House would no doubt presently create a new committee. The thousands of bills annually introduced are promptly distributed, therefore; go almost automatically to the several committees; and as automatically, it must be added, disappear. The measures reported to the House are measures which the committees formulate. They may find some member's bill suitable and acceptable, and report it substantially unchanged, or they may pull it about and alter it, or they may throw it aside altogether and frame a measure of their own, or they may do nothing, make no report at all. Few bills ever see the light again after being referred to a committee. The business of the House is what the committees choose to make it. What the House of Commons depends upon its committee, the Government, to do, the House depends upon its fifty-seven committees to do. The private member's bill has a little better chance, indeed, of being debated in the Commons than in the House of Representatives. The House of Commons does usually set aside one day a week for the consideration of private members' bills, when the Government is not pressed for time and does not insist upon using every day itself; and those members who are fortunate enough to draw first places in the makeup of the calendars for those days may have the pleasure of getting their proposals debated and voted upon. But in the House of Representatives there is only the very slender chance of getting the rules suspended, an irregularity which the businesslike chamber has grown very shy of permitting.

The very complexity and bulk of all this machinery is

itself burdensome to the House. There are now more. than half as many committees in the House as there are members in the Senate. It cannot itself choose so many committees; it cannot even follow so many. It therefore intrusts every appointment to the Speaker, and, when its business gets entangled amongst the multitude of committees and reports, follows a steering committee, which it calls the Committee on Rules. And the power of appointing the committees, which the House has conferred upon its Speaker, makes him the almost autocratic master of its actions.

In all legislative bodies except ours the presiding officer has only the powers and functions of a chairman. He is separate from parties and is looked to to be punctiliously impartial. He moderates and gives order to the course of debate, and is expected to administer without personal or party bias the accepted rules of its procedure. For political guidance all other representative assemblies depend on the Government, not upon committees which their presiding officer has created. But the processes of our parliamentary development have made the Speaker of our great House of Representatives and the Speakers of our State Legislatures party leaders in whom centres the control of all that they do. So far as the House of Representatives and its share in the public business is concerned, the Speaker is undisputed party leader.

Every one of the committees of the House the Speaker appoints. He not only allows himself to make them up with a view to the kind of legislation he wishes to see enacted; he is expected to make them up with such a view, — is expected to make them up as a party leader would. He is, it is true, a good deal hampered in the exercise of a free choice in their makeup by certain well-established understandings and precedents, of whose breach the older members of the House at any rate would be very jealous. Seniority of service has to be respected in assigning places on the more important committees, and the succession to certain of the chief chairmanships is well understood to go by definite rules of individual precedence and personal consideration. ⌊But⌋ it is always possible for the Speaker to determine the majority of his appointments in such a way as to give him that direct and continuing control of the actions of the House which he is now expected to exercise as the party leader of the majority.⌉ Even his own personal views upon particular public questions he does not hesitate to enforce in his appointments, so that the very majority he represents may be prevented from having an opportunity to vote upon measures it is known to desire because he has made up the committees which would report upon them in accordance with his own preferences in the matter. What the committees do not report the House cannot vote upon. Every bill that is introduced is assigned to a committee picked out by the Speaker's order, if there be any doubt about its character or reference. It is the Speaker's decision, also, that assigns the reports of the committees to the several calendars upon which the business of the House is allotted its time for consideration, and he may often choose whether the place allotted them shall be favorable or unfavorable, shall make it likely or unlikely that they will be reached at all.

Moreover, it has come about that by means of his prerogative of 'recognition' the Speaker is permitted to control debate to a very extraordinary degree. It is common parliamentary practice that no one can address an assembly until "recognized," that is, accorded the floor, by the presiding officer. The House of Representatives, feeling always pressed for time, even with regard to the consideration of the reports of its standing committees, which are numerous and amazingly active, restricts debate upon those reports within very narrow limits, and generally allots the greater part of the brief time allowed to any one report to the chairman of the reporting committee. Other members may get a few minutes of time allowed them by previous arrangement with the committee's chairman, and a list of those who are thus to be given an opportunity to speak generally lies on the Speaker's desk. These members the Speaker will "recognize," but no others, though they spring to their feet under his very nose in the open space in front of the seats, — unless, indeed, they have seen him beforehand and got his permission. No member who has not previously arranged the matter, either with the chairman of the committee or with the Speaker, need rise or seek to catch the Speaker's eye. And in the intervals of calendar business no one whose intention the Speaker has not been apprised of, unless indeed it be the leader on the floor of the one party or the other, may expect to be accorded the floor to make a motion. The Speaker may, if he choose, determine what proposals he will permit the House to hear.

The Committee on Rules has of recent years had a very singular and significant development of functions. Originally its duty was a very simple one: that of reporting to the House at the opening of each of its biennial sessions, when a new House assembles and a new organization is effected, the body of standing rules under which it was to

act; for the House goes through the form of readopting
its whole body of rules each time it reorganizes after fresh
congressional elections.   From session to session the rules
were modified, now in one particular, again in another, on
the recommendation of the committee; and any change
in the rules at any time proposed is still referred to it for
consideration and report.   But now the committee is
looked to, besides, for such temporary orders and programs
of procedure as will enable the House to disentangle its
business and get at the measures which the country expects it to dispose of or the needs of the Government make
it necessary that it should not neglect.   The party majority
is well aware that, if it would keep its credit with the
constituencies, it must not allow the miscellany of committee reports on its crowded calendars to stand in the
way of matters which it is pledged to act upon.   It looks
to the Committee on Rules to sweep aside the ordinary
routine of procedure whenever necessary, and bring in a
schedule of action which will enable it to get at the main
things it is interested in, or at any rate the things the party
leaders think it most expedient it should dispose of.   The
committee has thus become a very important part of party
machinery.   It consists of five members, the Speaker
himself, two other representatives of the majority, and
two representatives of the minority.   The majority members of course control its action; the representation of the
minority is hardly more than formal; and the two members of the majority associated with the Speaker upon it
are usually trusted lieutenants upon whom he can count
for loyal support of his leadership.   One self-confident
Speaker smilingly described the committee as consisting
of the Speaker and two assistants, — a pleasant way of

saying that the committee was his instrument to govern the House. His direct control of the Committee on Rules rounds out his powers as autocrat of the popular chamber.

And yet the word autocrat has really no place in our political vocabulary, if we are to use words of reality and not words of extravagance. The extraordinary power of the Speaker is not personal. He is in no proper sense of the word an autocrat. He is the instrument, as well as the leader, of the majority in controlling the processes of the House. He is obeyed because the majority chooses to be governed thus. The rules are of its own making, and it can unmake them when it pleases. It can override the Speaker's decisions, too, and correct its presiding officer as every other assembly can. It has simply found it most convenient to put itself in the Speaker's hands, its object being efficiency, not debate.

And yet it is also an exaggeration to say that House bills go through as the committees propose practically without debate. Some measures it is clearly in the interest of the party no less than of the public to discuss with some fullness. Many financial measures in particular are debated with a good deal of thoroughness, and most matters that have already attracted public attention. Not everything is left to the operation of the rules, the chances of the calendar, and the dictation of the Speaker and his two assistants. The Committee on Rules may be counted on to arrange for debates upon important bills as well as for putting unimportant bills out of the way.

And standing over all is the party caucus, the outside conference of the members of the majority, to whose conclusions the Speaker himself is subject, and to which members can appeal whenever they think the Speaker too irresponsible, too arbitrary, too masterful, too little heedful of the opinions prevalent on the floor among the rank and file. The caucus is an established and much respected piece of party machinery, and what the party has not the organization to decide on the floor of the assembly itself it decides in this conference outside the House. Members who do not wish to be bound by decisions of the caucus can refuse to attend it; but that is a very serious breach of party discipline and may get the men who venture upon it the unpleasant reputation of disloyalty. Members who wish to maintain their standing in the party are expected to attend; and those who attend are expected to abide by the decisions of the conference. It is a thorough-going means of maintaining party unity. Caucuses are free conferences, where a man may say what he pleases; but they are held behind closed doors, and it is usually made a matter of honorable punctilio not to speak outside of the dissensions their debates may have disclosed.

It is thus that the House has made itself "efficient." Its ideal is the transaction of business. It is as much afraid of becoming a talking shop as Mr. Carlyle could have wished it to be. If it must talk, it talks in sections, in its committee rooms, not in public on the floor of the chamber itself. The committee rooms are private. No one has the right to enter them except by express permission of the committees themselves. Not infrequently committees do hold formal public hearings with regard to certain bills, inviting all whose interests are affected to be represented and present their views either for or against the proposed legislation. But such hearings are recognized as exceptional, not of right, and as a rule the public hears nothing of the arguments which have induced any committee to make its particular recommendations to the House. The formal explanations of the chairman of a committee, made upon the floor of the House, contain few of the elements of contested opinion which undoubtedly showed themselves plainly enough in the private conferences of the committee.

For each committee is a miniature House. The minority is accorded representation upon it in proportion to its numerical strength in the House. In every committee, therefore, there are men representing both party views, and it sometimes happens that the arguments of the minority members are very influential in shaping reports made upon measures concerning which no sharp party lines have been drawn. With regard to matters upon which the majority is known to have taken a definite position before the constituencies the majority members of a committee will of course insist upon having their own way. They are apt to be in frequent consultation with the Speaker about them. But with regard to measures on which no party issue has been made up they are willing on occasion to give a good deal of weight to the opinions of their minority colleagues. There is a very easy and amicable relation between majority and minority in the committees, and it will often happen that in committees which have to deal with highly technical matters, like manufactures or banking or naval construction or the regulation of judicial procedure, or with matters involved in precedent and to be understood only in the light of somewhat extended and intimate experience, like foreign affairs, members of the minority of long service in the House and of long familiarity with the subject-matter under discussion will in fact in no small degree guide and dominate the committees to which they have been assigned. Business is more like

H

business, because less formal and less touched with party feeling, in the committee rooms than on the floor of the House.

The minority has its own party organization like that of the majority: its formally chosen leader for the floor, its caucus to secure common counsel. It is, indeed, usually less thoroughly disciplined than the majority, because it is in opposition, not in power, and can afford to allow its members freer play in choosing what they shall individually do and say. But its organization suffices to draw its forces together for common action when any matter of real party significance comes to the surface and the country expects it to put itself on record; and it is ready, at very short notice, to turn itself into an organization as complete and powerful as that of the majority, should the elections favor it and its leader become Speaker.

All lines of analysis come back to the Speaker, whether you speak of the organization or of the action and political power of the House. Such an organization, so systematized and so concentrated, has of course made the House of Representatives one of the most powerful pieces of our whole governmental machinery, and its Speaker, in whom its power is centered and summed up, has come to be regarded as the greatest figure in our complex system, next to the President himself. The whole powerful machinery of the great popular chamber is at his disposal, and all the country knows how effectually he can use it. Whatever may be the influence and importance of the Senate, its energies are not centered in any one man. There is no senator who sums up in himself the power of a great organ of government. The leaders of the Senate deal in all counsel with the other chamber with regard to legislative business with this single leader, this impersonation of the House. So do also the President and the members of the cabinet. As national leader of his party, the President must reckon always with the guide and master of the House, without whose approval and consent it is practically impossible to get any legislative measure adopted. Measures which are to prosper must have his countenance and support. Members of the cabinet must study his views and purposes, if they are to obtain the appropriations they desire or to see measures brought to a happy and successful issue which they deem necessary to the administration of their departments. One might sum up the active elements of our government as consisting of the President, with all his sweep of powers; the Speaker of the House, with all that he represents as spokesman of the party majority in the popular chamber, with its singularly effective machinery at his disposal; and the talkative, debating Senate, guided no doubt by a few influential and trusted members, but a council, not an organization.

The House of Commons makes and unmakes governments. The House of Representatives makes and unmakes Speakers. As the originative capacity of the House of Commons is exhausted when it has produced a ministry, so the originative force of the House of Representatives is exhausted when it has made a Speaker. Neither does anything else, as a whole. For the rest, they follow and criticize: follow fifty-seven committees or one committee; criticize the Speaker and his committees or the ministers who have risen to a place of rule. A numerous assembly cannot do more.

In producing a single committee and securing for it the right to conduct the government, the House of Commons has, it must be admitted, done a more effective thing than the House of Representatives has done in producing an omnipotent Speaker and fifty-seven committees, and has obtained for itself much greater power. There is reason to believe that the House of Representatives sometimes finds its numerous committees a burden, and certainly they do not all serve it equally well. The average membership of its standing committees is twelve, so that the total number of committee places to be filled is six hundred and eighty-five. The total membership of the House is only three hundred and fifty-seven. There are, therefore, about two committee places for every member of the House. The appointments are not equally distributed, but every member is given some place. New members and members little thought of can be disposed of on committees which have little or nothing to do or whose work is light and formal: for the House keeps many committees on its list for which it has ceased to have any real or important use; but with any sort of equitable distribution of the Speaker's appointments it must always happen that many committees with very important work to do are made up of men of only average capacity and little experience in public affairs. The real leaders and masters of business are few and are soon disposed of by assignment to the two or three chief committees; and to assign a man to a committee is practically to silence him with regard to every matter of legislation except those referred to his committee. A Speaker must have a particularly clear vision of what the most important questions to come before that particular congress are, to be able to distribute the best men at his disposal in the best way and give the House effective service where it will most need it. The membership of most committees must be drawn from the rank and file. The House can use its best men for only a few things, and must make shift for the rest with the mediocre.

Standing alone, therefore, and undertaking to be sufficient unto itself in respect of everything it is authorized by the Constitution to handle, the House of Representatives is a much less powerful and influential body than it would have been, could it have had the luck of the House of Commons and got control of the Government itself. Independence in any organization is isolation; and isolation is weakness. You have no controlling authority; you have only the right to sell your favors, to exchange concession for concession, to come to an agreement by some compromise of views. You can never have more than a piece of your own way. It is, of course, a more important and influential thing to superintend a Government with supreme authority, as the House of Commons does, than to stand separate in a complex organization, play only an individual part, be only a piece of a balanced mechanism, as the House of Representatives is. It is an interesting conclusion in political dynamics that a body which stands jealously apart and avoids partnership of any intimate sort in the conduct of affairs, declines an opportunity to rule and gets only an opportunity to bargain. If it is strong enough to rule, partnership will bring it supremacy; if it is not strong enough to rule, it can make little out of compromises and bargains. It is hardly to be expected that, as the affairs of the nation grow more complex and interesting and difficult and require nicer adjustments of governmental power for their management, the House of Representatives will remain content with its present splendid isolation.

We are in love with efficiency and, as a practical nation,

greatly admire the complete and thorough organization of the House, its preference for action and its impatience of talk: but if every part of our political machinery is to be organized for "business," where are counsel and criticism to come in? We never stood more in need of them than we do now. If our present representative assemblies are to be for action, we must let them go over in our thoughts to become outlying, detached parts of the executive, and must invent other assemblies for discussion. For public business cannot be transacted in a truly constitutional spirit without searching and constant discussion, unless we are mistaken in our analysis of constitutional government as government which is conducted in accordance with a clear understanding between those who administer it and those who obey it, — an understanding not only established by fundamental law, by charters and constitutions, but also accommodated to each day and generation by the criticisms and behests of representative assemblies whose business shall not be the actual discharge of governmental functions, but the maintenance of that nice balance between opinion and power which is of the very essence of the whole matter.

There is discussion and discussion. I suppose that we have come to think debate less necessary in our legislative assemblies than it may once have been because we have allowed ourselves to fancy that the action of government was sufficiently discussed and nicely enough squared with opinion by the news columns and editorials of our newspapers. But even if the chief newspapers were not owned by special interests; even if their utterances really spoke the general opinion of the communities in which they are printed, as very few of them now do, their discussion of affairs would not be of the kind that is necessary for the maintenance of constitutional government. There are many things to be said about the newspapers which will make this at once evident. For one thing, few men outside the big cities read more than one newspaper. Few men, therefore, ever get put before them in the newspapers they read more than one side of any question; and they generally decide for themselves beforehand which side that shall be, by their choice of a newspaper. But far more important than that is the little recognized fact that no number of separate discussions of a question, no matter how assembled, no matter from how many different points of view, from how many different papers or different sections of the country, constitute such a comparison of views as a responsible representative assembly can institute in its debates.

Discussions which are to lead to action must be combined, compounded, made up out of many elements, or else out of a few, by a process which can be thorough and trustworthy only when these several elements are, so to say, brought personally face to face, as living, contending forces embodied in men authorized to be the spokesmen of voters and speaking with a constant sense of being held responsible for what they say. Common counsel is not jumbled counsel. There is often common counsel in the committee rooms of the House, but there is never common counsel on the floor of the House itself. It goes without saying that the combined acts of a session are not a product of common counsel. They have been produced by a thousand agencies, not threshed out by one, and they have not been threshed out in the presence of the country, but behind closed doors.

It may sound a very subtle matter, but it is in fact intensely practical, and is worth looking into.  It is because we do not look into it or understand it, though it lies at the very heart of our whole practice of government, that we sometimes allow ourselves to assume that the "initiative" and the "referendum," now so much talked of and so imperfectly understood, are a more thorough means of getting at public opinion than the processes of our representative assemblies.  Many a radical program may get what will seem to be almost general approval if you listen only to those who know that they will not have to handle the perilous matter of action and to those who have merely formed an independent, that is, an isolated opinion, and have not entered into common counsel; but you will seldom find a deliberative assembly acting half so radically as its several members professed themselves ready to act before they came together into one place and talked the matter over and contrived statutes.  It is not that they lose heart or prove unfaithful to the promises made on the stump. They have really for the first time laid their minds alongside other minds of different views, of different experience, of different prepossessions.  They have seen the men with whom they differ, face to face, and have come to understand how honestly and with what force of genuine character and disinterested conviction, or with what convincing array of practical arguments opposite views may be held. They have learned more than any one man could beforehand have known.  Common counsel is not aggregate counsel.  It is not a sum in addition, counting heads.  It is compounded out of many views in actual contact; is a living thing made out of the vital substance of many minds, many personalities, many experiences; and it can be made up only by the vital contacts of actual conference, only in face to face debate, only by word of mouth and the direct clash of mind with mind.

No doubt, as I have said, there is oftentimes genuine common counsel in the committee rooms of the House of Representatives; but the committee rooms are private and are so many that it would only confuse the nation to publish debates out of the whole body of them. One could not make his way through a Congressional Record like that. And yet the actual Congressional Record is disappointing, because it seems to lack reality. The speeches it contains too often seem the mere speeches of parade; merely the formal dress array of arguments, so conned and formalized as not to seem like vital discussion at all, but only like things meant to have their effect by way of party justification or to make impressive reading for distant constituencies. In brief, the debate is not real hand to hand debate at all; and the people, finding things done they do not just know why or how in their legislative assemblies, indulge suspicions which deeply disturb them and make them unjust critics of the whole representative system. The process of legislation is not open and frank and obvious enough. Too much is hidden away in committee rooms. And anything hidden is suspected, no matter how honest it may be. The machinery of action is too complex to be easily understood. There are more excuses for suspecting covert influences than chances to comprehend what really takes place, — most of it in fact excellent, honest, practical, efficient enough.

It is very difficult for public opinion to judge such a body as the House of Representatives justly, because it is very difficult for it to judge it intelligently. If it cannot understand it, it will certainly be dissatisfied with it. Moreover, it is very difficult for a body which compounds its legislation by so miscellaneous a process as that of committees to bring itself into effective coöperation with the other parts of the government, — and synthesis, not antagonism, is the whole art of government, the whole art of power. I cannot imagine power as a thing negative, and not positive.

The matter is perfectly illustrated by the relations between the House and the Senate. They are not, it must be said, upon terms of very intimate and cordial coöperation. There is a subtle jealousy and antagonism between them, due to their desire to maintain their separateness and independence inviolate and be each a power to itself. When they come to a sharp difference of opinion upon any subject of legislation which really interests the people the advantage is sometimes with the one, sometimes with the other. The Senate has the advantage of being a public council, not a mere congeries of committees, and of setting forth its reasons in thorough debate; the House has the advantage of being regarded as the more truly representative chamber and of being more directly in touch with the general sentiment of the country. The House has also the advantage of being under thorough discipline and standing ready to do what it is told to do promptly when it becomes necessary to manœuvre for position in such a contest of wills. But what happens at last is proof of nothing, however the contest may end: it does not prove the popular sympathy of the House, if it win, nor the better counsel of the Senate, if it win. A conference committee is appointed by each house towards the very end of the session, the two committees meet and fight the differences of the houses out while business is hurrying to adjournment and a recess; and just as the session closes the two bodies hastily pass, without debate, a conference report which is a mere patchwork of compromises; or else reject the compromise and let the whole matter fall. There is no common leadership even when the majorities of the two houses are of the same political party. It is at best a haphazard method of compounding legislation, liable to suffer many singular accidents, and impossible for a busy people to understand when they occasionally look on with unwonted attention.

Such complications and subdivisions of machinery in the active and originative organs of the government result in its being in a very real sense leaderless. In the last lecture I spoke of the President as leader of his party and of the nation; but, though he clearly exercises such leadership, and exercises it with great effectiveness when he has the personal force for any originative rôle at all, he cannot be said to be the guide and leader of the Government as a whole. Our Government consists in part, as I have explained, of the House and Senate. It is in that respect contrasted with all other governments. And in each part of our subdivided Government there is a distinct arrangement with regard to leadership. The Senate submits to the guidance of a small group of senators, very jealous of the independence of the body they control. The House is under the command of its Speaker. The executive is in the hands of the President, whom the houses regard, when thinking of their own powers, as an outsider, and whose advice they are apt to look upon as the advice of a rival rather than of a colleague.

I suppose that when matters of legislation are under discussion the country is apt to think of the Speaker as the chief figure in Washington rather than the President, — at any rate in all ordinary seasons and under all ordinary Presidents. And yet, because he has the ear of the whole nation and is undoubtedly its chosen spokesman and representative, the President may place the House at a great disadvantage if he choose to appeal to the nation. It is this that makes the great difference between the Speaker and the President, whose figures you might come to regard as very nearly equal if you looked no farther than Washington city itself. The Speaker of the House is not in the habit of appealing to the nation. He would feel himself ridiculous if he did. It would probably make an unpleasant impression were the executive officer of one of the houses of Congress, himself merely the representative of a single constituency, to turn to the nation by some open appeal of speech or argument to decide between him and the President. It is a point of good taste with him, as well as of good politics, to say little, say that little in enigmatic phrases, and confine himself to his proper rôle of management. But the President may turn to the country when he will, with whatever arguments, whatever disclosures of plan, whatever explanations he pleases. Everybody will read what he says, particularly if there be any smack of contest in the air, while few will read what is said in the House where no one speaks for the whole body or for the nation; and if the nation happens to agree with the President, if he can win it to his view, the leadership is his whether the houses relish it or not. They are at a disadvantage and will probably have to yield.

The true significance of the matter, for any student of government who wishes to understand the life rather than

the mere theory of what he studies, is that the greatest
power lies with that part of the government which is in
most direct communication with the nation itself, — as one
would naturally expect under any constitutional system.
The light this evident fact throws upon the House of
Representatives is this: that it has greatly weakened
itself as an organ of public opinion by yielding to the need
it has felt itself under to play the rôle of an independent
part of the government. In its effort to make itself an
instrument of business, to perform its function of legislation without assistance or suggestion, to formulate its
own bills, digest its own measures, originate its own policies, it has in effect silenced itself. The nation does not
look to it for counsel; does not expect to understand its
own affairs any better because of anything said or anything
done in the House; has come to regard it as what it is, a
piece of effective law-making machinery, but not a deliberative assembly in whose debates it may expect to find public
questions clarified, disputed matters settled. The House
seems to have missed what its average capacity and its
undoubted integrity entitle it to, the chief privilege of
giving counsel to the nation, the right to be its principal
spokesman in affairs.

It is thus always a vital synthesis of parts that eludes
us as we examine our constitutional system with its
singular Newtonian equipoise of parts. But it is a study
of persons and of forces of opinion, as in any other government. It is the actual temper and disposition of the two
diverse chambers with which he deals that the President
must study if he is to bring his party, as well as the
opinion of the nation, to any program or measure of his
own. The Senate and House must study one another and

play a very difficult game of accommodation to maintain any workable agreement or coöperation in legislation. They are of different tempers and traditions; they are jealous of each other and yet are constrained to agree. No man can lay down any rule as to what will happen amidst so many and so powerful forces, which must coöperate and yet are independent of one another. Time and circumstance and wise management alone can secure union and energy among them. There is but one common solvent. The law of their union is public opinion. That and that alone can draw them together. That part of the government, therefore, which has the most direct access to opinion has the best chance of leadership and mastery; and at present that part is the President.

Each part of the government loses force and prestige in proportion as it ceases to give, and to give publicly, conclusive reasons for what it is doing and for what it is declining to do. The country in the long run is more interested to know that the right thing has been done and that it has been done wisely than to know merely that something has been done, hastily devised though well intended. There are seasons, it is true, when opinion, unduly excited, prefers action to counsel, but those are exceptional seasons among peoples trained to the thoughtfulness and self-control of constitutional action. Open counsel is of the essence of power, if the country's confidence is to be retained for any length of time. The most serious comment, therefore, upon the development of the House of Representatives is that in making itself an active part of the Government and falling into the silence of an effective, businesslike board of directors, it has forfeited the much higher office of gathering the common counsel of the nation and wielding the tremendous, the governing and sovereign, power of criticism. Criticism can make and unmake governments, but the conferences of committee rooms cannot. If the House must originate its own business and must be independent in action, it cannot be the voice of the nation.

# V

## THE SENATE

IT is very difficult to form a just estimate of the Senate of the United States. No body has been more discussed; no body has been more misunderstood and traduced. There was a time when we were lavish in spending our praises upon it. We joined with our foreign critics and appreciators in speaking of the Senate as one of the most admirable, as it is certainly one of the most original, of our political institutions. In our own day we have been equally lavish of hostile criticism. We have suspected it of every malign purpose, fixed every unhandsome motive upon it, and at times almost cast it out of our confidence altogether.

The fact is that it is possible in your thought to make almost anything you please out of the Senate. It is a body variously compounded, made many-sided by containing many elements, and a critic may concentrate his attention upon one element at a time if he chooses, make the most of what is good and put the rest out of sight, or make more than the most of what is bad and ignore everything that does not chime with his thesis of evil. The Senate has, in fact, many contrasted characteristics, shows many faces, lends itself easily to no confident generalization. It differs very radically from the House of Representatives. The House is an organic unit; it has been at great pains to make itself so, and to become a working body under a single unifying discipline; while the Senate is not so much an organization as a body of individuals, retaining with singularly little modification the character it was originally intended to have.

As I have already said in a previous lecture, it is impossible to characterize the United States in any single generalization; and for that very reason it is impossible to sum up the Senate in any single phrase or summary description. For the Senate is as various as the country it represents. It represents the country, not the people: the country in its many diverse sections, not the population of the country, which tends to become uniform where it is concentrated.

Most of the leading figures among the active public men of the country are now to be found in the Senate, not in the House. This was not formerly the case. Before the House became an effective, non-debating organ of business, it shared quite equally with the Senate the leading politicians of the country; but it has not been so of recent years. Organization swallows men up, debate individualizes them, and men of strong character and active minds always prefer the position in which they will be freest to speak and act for themselves. The Senate has always been a favorite goal of ambition for our public men, but it has become more and more the place of their preference as the House has more and more surrendered to it the function of public counsel.

Of course, there are fewer senators than members of the House, and it is a more conspicuous thing to be one of a body of ninety than to be one of a body of three hundred and fifty-seven. Moreover, the tenure of a senator of the United States is three times as long as the tenure of a

I

member of the House of Representatives, and every member of the Senate must feel it a considerable advantage that six years instead of two are given him in which to make his impression on the country. There is time to find out what he is about and to master a difficult task. Both the smaller membership of the Senate and the longer term of its members contribute to individualize the men who compose it and to give them an advantage and importance which members of the House do not often have, unless they rise to one of the three or four places of real power which crown the committee organization of the representative chamber.

And yet these are not the radical and fundamental differences between the House and the Senate. Size and tenure are after all matters of detail. They count, and count a good deal, in giving the Senate its character, but they do not go to the root of the difference between the two houses. What gives the Senate its real character and significance as an organ of constitutional government is the fact that it does not represent population, but regions of the country, the political units into which it has, by our singular constitutional process, been cut up. The Senate, therefore, represents the variety of the nation as the House does not. It does not draw its membership chiefly from those parts of the country where the population is most dense, but draws it in equal parts from every state and section.

It seems to me that those critics of our government — they are, I believe, without exception domestic critics — who criticize the principle upon which the Senate is made up on the ground that states having little wealth and small population have as many representatives in the Senate as the richest and most populous states of the

Union, the newest and least developed as many as the oldest and most highly organized, entirely mistake the standard by which the Senate should be judged as an instrumentality of constitutional government in a system like ours.

They are entirely wrong in assuming, for one thing, that the newer, weaker, or more sparsely populated parts of the country have less of an economic stake in its general policy and development than the older states and those which have had a great industrial development. Their stake may not be equal in dollars and cents, — that, of course, — but it is probably greater in all that concerns opportunity and the chances of life. There is a sense in which the interest of the poor man in the prosperity of the country is greater than that of the rich man: he has no reserve, and his very life may depend upon it. The very life of an undeveloped community may depend upon what will cause a richer community mere temporary inconvenience or negligible distress. And yet even this, vital as it is to the validity of the usual criticisms of the make-up and character of the Senate, is in fact neither here nor there as compared with the essential point of the matter.

Neither is it of material consequence that some of the states represented in the Senate are not real communities, with distinct historical characteristics, a distinct social and economic character of their own, as most of the older states are. It is true that you have only to look at a map of the United States to see at a glance that many of the newer states of the Union are purely arbitrary creations, their boundaries established by the theodolite of the public surveyor. They are squares on a great checker-board, elaborated into rectangular sections on broad plains where there are no natural boundaries to divide region from region; and these artificial squares, which Congress first laid off as the areas of territories, it has one by one converted into states, each of which sends two members to the Senate, just as Virginia and Massachusetts do, the history of whose boundaries and organization is a long history of constitutional struggle which gave them from the very outset characters and purposes of their own. Many a square western state, laid out by the public surveyor, has now a more homogeneous population and a more discernible individuality than some of her eastern sisters into whom a miscellaneous immigration has poured social chaos. And their very separateness of political organization insures them a development of their own.

Yet even that is not of material consequence. Even if every state of the Union were of artificial creation, not a natural community, but merely a region marked off to make a congressional district for elections to the Senate, the principle I am just now interested in pointing out as of capital importance in a system and country like ours would not be altered or affected. That is the principle that regions must be represented, irrespective of population, in a country physically as various as ours and therefore certain to exhibit a very great variety of social and economic and even political conditions. It is of the utmost importance that its parts as well as its people should be represented; and there can be no doubt in the mind of any one who really sees the Senate of the United States as it is that it represents the country, as distinct from the accumulated populations of the country, much more fully and much more truly than the House of Representatives does. The East and North are regions of concentration, regions of teeming population and highly developed industry, — the regions north of Mason and Dixon's Line and east of the Mississippi. It will not long be so. Cities are springing up in the South and beyond the Mississippi in the Middle West, on the Pacific coast, and upon the great lines of traffic that connect coast with coast, which will presently rival the cities of the East and of the old Northwest in magnitude and importance; and many a region hitherto but sparsely peopled is thickening apace with crowding settlers and an accumulating commerce. But for the present the South and West, if I may use those terms in the large, are not the centres of wealth or of population, and have a character unlike that of the marts of trade and industry; and there are more senators from the South and West than from the North and East. The House of Representatives tends more and more, with the concentration of population in certain regions, to represent particular interests and points of view, to be less catholic and more and more specialized in its view of national affairs. It represents chiefly the East and North. The Senate is its indispensable offset, and speaks always in its make-up of the size, the variety, the heterogeneity, the range and breadth of the country, which no community or group of communities can adequately represent. It cannot be represented by one sample or by a few samples; it can be represented only by many, — as many as it has parts.

It thus happens that there are in the Senate more representatives of the individual parts of the country than of the characteristic parts of it. At least that is true if I am right in assuming that the characteristic parts of America are those parts which are most highly developed, where population teems and great communities are quick with industry, where our life most displays its energy, its ardor of enterprise, its genius for material achievement. Other communities are no doubt more truly characteristic of America as she has been known in the processes of her making. Only modern visitors, visitors of our own day, have known her as industrial America, the leader of the world in all the processes, whether material or economic, which produce wealth and accumulate power, the land of manufactures and of vast cities. The older America is still represented by the South and West with their simpler life, their more scattered people, their fields of grain, their mines of metal, their little towns, their easier pace of intercourse, their work that does not crowd out companionship.

Certainly it is easier to represent a northern or eastern constituency in Congress than to represent a southern or western constituency. There is more individuality, man for man, in the West and South than in the East and North. How constantly we repeat each other's opinions and bow to each other's influence; how seldom we take leave to be ourselves and utter thoughts of our own genuine coinage, in regions where we are parts of a packed and thronging multitude! Rubbing shoulders every day with thousands of your fellow-citizens, putting your mind into contact with other minds at every encounter, you slowly have the individuality rubbed out of you by mere attrition and are worn down to a common pattern. Your opinion is everybody's opinion; my information is the common information current everywhere: your mind, like mine, like our neighbor's, is assaulted day and night with the multitudinous voices of clamorous talk, and a common atmosphere gives us a common habit and attitude. Only very unusual men can remain individual under such pressure of uniformity. It is uncomfortable to be singular in any habit, whether of action or of thought, where so many look on and make comment. Conformity is the easiest, plainest, safest way, and countless multitudes there be that walk in it. "Always be of the opinion of the person with whom you are conversing," was Dean Swift's advice to all who would win the repute of being sensible persons. And in crowded places of enterprise it is a very valuable asset of success to be thus reputed a man of sense. To conform opens the ways to promotion. It is the common and very uncomfortable fortune of men of original views to be greeted at every turn with a stare and a shrug of the shoulders, as Mr. Bagehot has said, and to be followed with the comment, "An excellent young man, sir, but unsafe, quite unsafe." Mr. Bagehot must certainly have known: he was himself most singularly original and seemed always to have had the freshness of youth about him.

The variety of the country, therefore, is better represented in the Senate than in the House, its variety of opinion as well as its variety of social and economic make-up, — its variety of opinion because its variety of social and economic make-up. There are more opinions because there is more individuality in the uncrowded South and West than in the crowded East and North. Each mind is there apt to have a greater, freer space about it, space in which to look around and form impressions of its own. No country ought ever to be judged from its seething centres. To be truly known, it must be known where it is quiet, in places where impulse is not instant, hot, insistent; where you can at least presume that opinion will next week be what it is to-day.

In those hot centres of trade and industry, where a man's business grips him like an unrelaxing hand of iron from morning to night and lies heavily upon him even while he sleeps, few men can be said to have any opinions at all. They may bury their heads for a few minutes in the morning paper at breakfast or as they hurry to their offices, may dwell with dull attention upon the afternoon paper as they go wearily home again or drowse after dinner; but what they get out of the papers they cannot call their opinions. They are not opinions, but merely a miscellany of mental reactions, never assorted, never digested, never made up into anything than can for the moment compare in reality and vitality with the energetic conceptions they put to use in their business. In small towns, in rural country-sides, around comfortable stoves in cross-road stores, wherever business shows as many intervals as transactions, where seasons of leisure alternate with seasons of activity, where large undertakings wait on slow, unhasting nature, where men are neighbors and know each other's quality, where politics is dwelt upon in slow talk with all the leisure and fond elaboration usually bestowed on gossip, where discussion is as constant a pastime as checkers, opinion is made up with an individual flavor and wears all the variety of individual points of view. And the Senate has more members from such regions than from those where opinion is made up by conglomeration and upon the moment, out of newspapers and not out of the contributions of individual minds. It represents the population of the country, not in its numbers, but in its variety; and it is of the utmost consequence that the country's variety should be represented as thoroughly as its mass.

The processes by which we have made states out of

the territories of the United States have been seriously
impaired once and again by mistakes which are the more
to be deplored because they are apparently irremediable.
Once make a state and you cannot unmake it. Once or
twice Congress has admitted to the Union, in equal partnership with the older states, territories which not only did
not have population enough to justify their admission,
but which had no real prospect of gaining a population
large and various enough to develop into compact and important communities with a character and purpose of their
own, — communities already sufficiently represented in
kind in the counsels of the country, and not constituted
in a way which gave promise of political vitality. But
such mistakes have been few, and many a state which at
first seemed a premature and unjustifiable creation has
been speedily lifted to a plane of real dignity and importance by the abounding forces of our national growth.
It has been hard to make mistakes where populations
throng forward so steadily and in such wholesome masses
to occupy the free spaces of the continent. We have
had to reclaim deserts to accommodate their multitude.
And as each new-fledged state has come in, its two spokesmen in the Senate have added its voice to our counsels
in a place where voices can still be individually heard.

The fact that the Senate has kept its original rules of
debate and procedure substantially unchanged, is very
significant. It is a place of individual voices. The sup-
pression of any single voice would radically change its
constitutional character; and, its character being changed,
the individual voices of the country's several regions being
silenced, there would no longer be any sufficient reason
for its present constitution. If it were to follow the ex-

ample of the House and make itself chiefly an efficient organ for the transaction of business, the critics who condemn it because it is unequally compounded upon any balanced reckoning of the wealth and numbers of the country would have not a little tenable ground to stand upon.

Another circumstance gives a senator of the United States an individual importance which the average member of the House of Representatives lacks. He comes into contact with a much greater variety of the public business. He is not a mere legislator. He is directly associated with the President in some of the most delicate and important functions of government. He is a member of a great executive council. He is brought into very confidential relations with the President in matters which oftentimes call for not a little discretion and for very prudent judgments, — judgments not to be drawn from public opinion, but only from official facts privately considered, not spoken of out of doors, belonging to intimate counsel and not to public debate. There is no better cure for thinking disparagingly of the Senate than a conference with men who belong to it, to find how various, how precise, how comprehensive their information about the affairs of the nation is; and to find, what is even more important, how fair, how discreet, how regardful of public interest they are in the opinions which they will express in your private ear.

The most reticent men in Washington are the members of the Supreme Court of the United States. It would of course be a great breach of professional honor on the part of any member of that Court to discuss any question involved in a pending case which the Court was considering or was about to consider; but his obligation of reticence goes much farther than that. Almost any piece of public policy that touches the individual, though it be never so indirectly, may sooner or later come before the Supreme Court for judicial examination. Every member of the Court, therefore, feels bound to keep his opinions upon such matters to himself. He will not discuss with you any but the most general public questions, holds discreetly silent with regard to every mooted matter of legal policy or construction. Men who know the proprieties never broach such matters with members of the Court. Senators feel a similar obligation of honor with regard to the matters in which they bear a confidential relation to the executive. They are not at liberty to state to you or even to their constituents at home the grounds for such action as they may have taken in executive sessions of the Senate until the whole matter is so long gone by that no possible harm or embarrassment can come of publicity with regard to it. Members of the House are not under such restraints. Nothing comes before the House of Representatives which it is not the right of every man in the United States to discuss if he will. No doubt members sometimes act upon private information from the White House or a department which they would feel it unwise to make generally known; but that seldom happens, and if the House talked at all, it might talk about anything it chose that it had information enough to understand.

It is no essential part of our present study to ask by what influences either members of the House or members of the Senate obtain their seats. That is a question concerning, not the form and purpose of our political institutions, but the moral character of the nation itself, the social influences which work in it for good or evil. But so much has been said in recent years about the methods by which seats in the Senate are secured, so much that is of evil report has been believed, that the question cannot be passed by without giving our whole inquiry the appearance of a lack of candor. And, after all, any serious loss of prestige it may suffer must greatly impair the Senate's power and influence, its usefulness as an instrument of constitutional government. It has become customary to speak of it as a rich man's club, and any writer who professes to adduce proofs that the corporate interests of the country, the great railroads and the greater trusts, have secured virtual control of it by putting into it men of their own choice, engaged in their behalf by one of influence or another to block any legislation likely to harm them, gains easy credence. Where there is so much smoke, must there not be a little fire? It is a question which touches the integrity of our whole constitutional system. It would be affectation to avoid it.

There are many opinions as to the way in which men obtain seats in the Senate; and I dare say that for every opinion there is a corresponding method, — not just the method suggested by the opinion, but sufficiently like it to give the opinion more than plausible color. There are many ways of getting into the Senate. There are some very bad ways; some ways that are neither bad nor good; and some very good ways. What it interests me most to observe with regard to the matter, in view of what I have just been saying of the make-up of the Senate and its general relation to the country, is that, so far as one may judge from rumor and from what appears in the public prints, the bad ways have been oftenest illustrated where population is thickest and in a few of the recently created states, which, because of their peculiar economic character, are dominated by a single interest or a single group of interests. They have not often been illustrated, to be more specific, in those normal western and southern states, which I have spoken of in contrast with the centres of population and industry as standing for the nation's variety, characteristic of its rich diversity alike of quality and of interest rather than of its accumulations of wealth and of material power.

The purchasing power of money in politics is chiefly exerted where there is most money. The selfish influence of great corporations is most often exhibited where they have their seats of control, at the financial centres of the country. The processes by which men procure places in the Senate have been most often under suspicion where men buy most things. One is forced to believe that there are some communities, even in the America which we love, where the dollar is god, where everything is estimated in money value, and where actual cash is paid for votes; and unquestionably there are other communities in which the highest political preferment has sometimes been bought, not by the direct use of money, but by means equally demoralizing, — perhaps more demoralizing because less obviously venal, — by a covert bartering of favors, unspoken promises, business opportunities offered and accepted without any sign given of aught but kindly interest and natural friendship. But the whole country knows the cases in which these things are suspected, and knows them to be few. No candid man who knows anything of the character and circumstances of the persons whose names he reads can look through the roll of the Senate and think for a moment that such influences predominate there.

In order to get a correct impression of the Senate, it is necessary that you extend your observation beyond particular sections of the country. One of the greatest disadvantages that public opinion labors under in the United States is that we have no national newspaper, no national organ of opinion. There is no newspaper in the United States which is not local, and narrowly local at that, both in the news which it prints and in the views which it expresses. Each paper makes such selections of general news as will interest the particular locality in which it is printed, and expresses such views of the nation's affairs as local interest or information suggest. If you read New York papers, you will have New York opinions; if you read Philadelphia papers, you will have Philadelphia opinions; if you read Chicago papers, you will have Chicago opinions; if you read San Francisco papers, you will have, not western, but merely San Franciscan, opinions. And if you read papers from all four cities, you will not get national opinion. Though the impressions they give you may sometimes seem to have the air of being national, you will find that they are after all local impressions, though made up out of national material. They bear the color of a place. I dare say the thing is inevitable in so big a country; but undoubtedly one of the reasons why we so habitually misjudge the Senate of the United States is that we have no national medium of intelligence, and the papers most widely read reflect not national, but local, conditions.

Indeed, one of the serious difficulties of politics in this country, whether you look at it from the point of view of the student or the point of view of the statesman, is its provincialism, — the general absence of national information and, by the same token, of national opinion. And one is forced to believe, reluctantly enough if he live in the East, that the East is the most provincial part of the Union, — a very serious matter, because most of our information and most of our opinion is printed in the East and transmitted thence. The East, being the oldest part of the country, having been for a long time the whole of it, having the oldest roots of history, the longest traditions of influence, the greatest wealth and hitherto an unquestioned command of the economic development of the whole country, shows as yet little intimate consciousness of the rest of it; is much less aware of other communities and other interests than its own than are other parts of the country. The chief reason why the President of the United States can concentrate in himself, if he choose, greater power and a more extended influence than any other person or any other group of persons connected with the government, is, as I have already several times pointed out, that all the country is curious about him and interested in him as our one national figure, eager to hear everything that emanates from him. His doings and sayings constitute the only sort of news that is invariably transmitted to every corner of the country and read with equal interest in every sort of neighborhood. He is the one person about whom a definite national opinion is formed and, therefore, the one person who can form opinion by his own direct influence and act upon the whole country at once.

It has, therefore, too often escaped the attention of the country as a whole that the large majority of the members of the Senate of the United States obtain their seats by perfectly legitimate methods, because the people whom they represent honestly prefer them as representatives; that the large majority of them are poor men who have little or nothing to live on besides their inadequate salaries; that the opinion and action of the Senate are for the most part determined by the influence of quiet men whom the country talks about very little and about whom it suspects nothing in the least questionable or dishonorable; and that the few notorious members whose reputations are most talked of generally play but a very obscure part in its business. In most of the states great corporations, great combinations of interest, have little to do with the choice of senators. Men go to the Senate who are in a very real sense the choice of the people, — or rather men to whom natural and genuine political leadership has come by reason of their personal force or of their services to their party, — men of the rank and file who have made their way to the top by political, not by commercial, means, and who enjoy a veritable popular support. There are one or two very influential members of the Senate who are also very rich men; but they are influential, not because of their riches, but because of their long and intelligent service, their complete experience in affairs, and the relations of intimate personal confidence which they have established with their fellow senators. You have but to make the most casual inquiries in Washington to ascertain that the men who are in fact most influential in the proceedings of the Senate are not the men most advertised in the newspapers, most conspicuous in the talk of the Capitol, not the men who talk most effectively for those far-off "galleries" which lie away from Washington, but small groups of quiet gentlemen seldom spoken of in the public prints, more thoughtful of their duties than of being generally talked about, — men who have not laid by fortunes, but who have been at the pains to grow rich in the esteem of the fellow citizens at home who know and support them.

One of the present difficulties lying in the way of maintaining a high grade of excellence in the Senate, as in the House, is that we do not pay our representatives in either house salaries large enough to command men of the best abilities, or even sufficiently to support those who accept seats in the houses, in the sort of domestic comfort and dignity we naturally expect them to maintain. Men of the highest ability do accept seats in the House and Senate, but they do so generally at a great sacrifice, find it exceedingly difficult to live in so expensive a place as Washington without a very teasing economy, and are usually forced at last to seek some remunerative employment in order to pay the debts they have almost inevitably accumulated in serving a country which economizes in the wrong items of its budget. If the Senate should ever come to deserve in fact the reputation of being a rich men's club, the true cause will be found rather in the salary account on our national budget than in the power of wealth to buy legislative seats. As it stands now, only rich men can afford, if they be in love with self-respecting ways of living, to accept an election in the Senate.

This, then, is the Senate, the House of individuals, a body of representative American men, representing the many elements of the nation's make-up, exhibiting the vitality of a various people, speaking for the several parts of a country of many parts and many interests, a whole and yet full of sharp social and political contrasts; men much above the average in ability and in personal force; men connected in most cases by long service with the business of the government and accustomed to handle

K

its affairs in all their range and variety; a body of counselors who act, if not always wisely or without personal and party bias, yet always with energy and without haste.

It is interesting to the looker-on in Washington to observe the unmistakable condescension with which the older members of the Senate regard the President of the United States. Dominate the affairs of the country though he may, he seems to them at most an ephemeral phenomenon. Even if he has continued in his office for the two terms which are the traditional limit of the President's service, he but overlaps a single senatorial term by two years, and a senator who has served several terms has already seen several Presidents come and go. His experience of affairs is much mellower than the President's can be; he looks at policies with a steadier vision than the President's; the continuity of the government lies in the keeping of the Senate more than in the keeping of the executive, even in respect of matters which are of the especial prerogative of the presidential office. A member of long standing in the Senate feels that he is the professional, the President an amateur.

I have dwelt at some length upon the character and the true constitutional purpose of the Senate because that character and purpose govern its whole organization and action. It is as different from the House in organization as in character and constitutional position. Its power is not concentrated in its presiding officer as the power of the House is. On the contrary, its presiding officer is of all its constituent parts the least significant. In mere fact, the Vice President of the United States is, in any analysis of the powers and activities of the Senate, practically negligible. Some occupants of that singular office

have, it is true, made a considerable impression upon the
Senate and have left distinct marks of their individuality
upon its record, particularly in matters of procedure.
Men of great natural force and unusual personality cannot
spend four years in the chair of so serious and so busy an
assembly without leaving some memory of their influence.
But the Vice Presidents of the United States have, almost
without exception, whatever their natural vigor or instinct
of initiative, felt that their relation to the Senate was
purely formal. The Vice President is not a member of
the Senate. His duties are only the formal and altogether
impartial duties of a presiding officer. His position
seems to demand that he should take no part in party
tactics and should hold carefully aloof from all parliamentary struggles for party advantage. Its very dignity
seems to rob it of vitality in respect of the only duties
assigned to it by the Constitution. And yet the president
*pro tempore* of the Senate, the Vice President's substitute
upon occasion, is a vital political figure. He is chosen
by his party associates of the majority to play a real part
in the business of the assembly. He holds office at the
pleasure of the Senate and is in a much more intimate
and sympathetic relation with the party he represents
than the Vice President of the United States can be.

Once or twice it has looked as if the president *pro tempore*
were likely to accumulate powers and prerogatives which
might give his office a power and authority comparable
with those of the Speaker of the House of Representatives.
The Senate, like the House, prepares its business through
the instrumentality of standing committees, and in 1828
it conferred upon its president *pro tempore* the authority
to appoint its committees. But in 1833, for political

reasons which it is not necessary to detail here, it again changed its rule and resumed to itself the right to constitute its committees by its own choice by ballot. Again in 1837 it turned to the president *pro tempore* for relief and conferred upon him the power of appointment, the balloting having proved very cumbersome and burdensome; but in 1845 circumstances again compelled it to withdraw the authority. Many considerations seem to render the president *pro tempore* unavailable for such functions. The statute of 1792 had put the president *pro tempore* of the Senate in the line of succession to the presidency of the United States in case of a vacancy, providing that if both President and Vice President should die or become disqualified, the president *pro tempore* of the Senate should assume the duties of the presidency. The Senate regarded its president *pro tempore*, therefore, as a necessary officer only in order that there should be no lapse in the office of President. It chose him only for the occasions when the Vice President was absent from his chair, and allowed his office to lapse again upon the Vice President's return. But a change in the law governing the succession to the presidency altered the whole character of the temporary office. In 1886 a new statute vested the succession in the heads of the executive departments, in an order of precedence determined by the dates at which their several offices had been created, and the president *pro tempore* of the Senate was omitted from the line of succession. Ten years before the Senate had decided that its president *pro tempore* need not be regarded as merely a temporary officer chosen from time to time upon the occasion of each absence of the Vice President from its sittings, and in 1890 it confirmed its decision in that respect and extended the tenure of this officer of its own choice indefinitely. He now holds at the pleasure of the Senate, takes the chair whenever the Vice President happens to be absent, and is superseded only by the election of some one else in his place. He is appointed to many important committees of the Senate like any ordinary member, is usually himself chairman of a leading committee, and is always sure to be one of the chief figures of his party on the floor. Upon a change of majority his office lapses and a successor is chosen from the new majority.

And yet, singularly enough, though he has grown in importance with the permanence of his office and has seemed once and again to be chosen as in some sense the leading representative of his party in the chamber, as the Speaker of the House is, he is not in fact in command in debate or in the direction of party tactics. [The leader of the Senate is the chairman of the majority caucus.] Each party in the Senate finds its real, its permanent, its effective organization in its caucus, and follows the leadership, in all important parliamentary battles, of the chairman of that caucus, its organization and its leadership alike resting upon arrangements quite outside the Constitution, for which there is no better and no other sanction than human nature.

[The Senate, like the House, digests and manages its business through standing committees, and the appointment of those committees it has in large measure kept in its own hands.] But the old method of actually choosing them by ballot it has not found it convenient or even possible to maintain. Its machinery for the selection of committees, as for other party purposes, is the caucus. The caucus of each party has its Committee on Committees, appointed by its chairman, subject to the ratification of the caucus itself, and charged with the important function of selecting its party's representatives on the standing committees. The majority caucus has, besides, its Steering Committee, similarly appointed, to which fall duties very like those of the Committee on Rules in the House.

The chairman of the majority caucus is much more nearly the counterpart of the Speaker of the House than is the president *pro tempore*. His influence is very great and very pervasive. Through the Committee on Committees and the Steering Committee, both of which he appoints subject to the confirmation of the caucus, he plays no small part in determining both the character and the handling of the business the Senate is called on to consider.

[But the Senate is a deliberative assembly and is under no such discipline of silence and obedience to its committees as the House is.] The duties of its committees are much more like those of ordinary old-fashioned committees such as are usually found in all parliamentary bodies, than are the duties of the House committees. They are by no means in complete control of the business of the Senate. A bill introduced by an individual senator may be put upon the calendar, debated, and voted upon without reference to a committee at all. The committees are an imperative convenience, and the greater part of the Senate's business is of course prepared by them; but they are not permitted to monopolize the floor, and the chamber is quick to recognize the right of its individual members to have their proposals considered directly, without committee intervention.

Moreover, the make-up of the committees of the Senate

is determined much more strictly by seniority and by personal privilege and precedence than is the membership of the committees of the House, with much less regard to party lines and much more regard to personal and sectional considerations, — by equitable arrangement rather than by the personal choice or individual purpose of the caucus chairmen. The variety of the country is allowed to show itself in the constitution of its committees, as in its debates and its recognition of individual privilege among its members. An old-fashioned air of equality and democracy is still perceptible in the Senate, its popular reputation to the contrary notwithstanding, — something of the discipline of party whips and leaders, as must in any political assembly be inevitable, but much more of the air of debate, much less the air of rigidly organized business and mere efficiency, than in the popular chamber.

Indeed, the Senate is, *par excellence*, the chamber of debate and of individual privilege. Its discussions are often enough unprofitable, are too often marred by personal feeling and by exhibitions of private interest which taint its reputation and render the country uneasy and suspicious, but they are at least the only means the country has of clarifying public business for public comprehension. When we turn to the question which is the central question of our whole study, the question of the coördination of the Senate with the other organs of the government and the synthesis of authority and power for common action, it at once becomes evident that such a body as I have described the Senate to be, must be very hard indeed to digest into any system. A coördination of wills, united movement under a common leadership, is of the very essence of every efficient form of government. The Senate has a very stiff will of its own, a pride of independent judgment, very admirable in itself, but not calculated to dispose it to prompt accommodation when it differs in its views and objects from the House or the President. Its very excellences stand in its way as an organ of coöperation: its slow deliberation, its tolerance of individual opinion, its confidence in the political judgment and experience of its own leaders, the feeling of permanency and stability which seems to lift it a little above the influences of the immediate day, the critical moment of decision. It looks upon the House of Representatives very much as it looks upon the President, — as an organ of opinion, indeed, and as a coördinate branch of the government of undoubted commission from the people, but as likely to change, a thing that, in its present character and disposition at least, is here to-day and gone to-morrow, to make room for new men and new moods.

The membership of the House is much less stable than the membership of the Senate. Not only is the term of a senator three times as long as the term of a member of the House, but members of the House are much less often reëlected than are members of the Senate. Most states are content to continue their senators in their seats for long periods together, but few congressional districts can be counted upon not to change their choice very frequently. Not only does the *personnel* of the House change rapidly and the *personnel* of the Senate change very slowly, but the party majority is much more often changed in the one than in the other. For a great many years now the leaders of our national parties have been obliged to think of the country as one thing when considered with a view to the make-up of the Senate, and another thing when considered with a view to the make-up of the House. Parties have often changed places in commanding the majority in the House during the last fifty years, but not often in the Senate. The people reckoned by states have usually preferred the Republican party; the people reckoned by numbers have turned in their choice of men and of parties first to the one party and then to the other, as men and programs have changed.

All this, of course, has its effect upon the temper of the Senate. It is less disturbed by elections than the House is, feels itself in great part sheltered from the winds of party contest, and is apt to look upon itself as the poise and makeweight of the whole system, which might swing into an erratic orb were it allowed to yield to the impulses of changing opinion too rapidly. And it is confirmed in this view of its functions by the character of its leaders. It must be said that the method by which leaders are made in the Senate is much more normal, much more in the course of nature, than the method by which they are made in the House. Nature intended that leaders should be self-selected, by proof given of their actual quality in the business in which they aspire to lead. And since leaders of the Senate are expected to lead in counsel, they are generally men proved by counsel, men of long training in public affairs who have been under inspection by their fellow members for many sessions together. The Senate is inclined to follow its veterans, — not necessarily its chief debaters, but the men who by long service have gained a full experience and, by many evidences of good sense and cool judgment, the entire confidence of their party associates, as guides who will not blunder. The leaders of the House win their places by service on the floor, no doubt,

before being made Speakers, but they win them as masters
of parliamentary tactics and as men of will and resource
rather than as men of counsel; and they win them in a
restless and changeful assembly few of whose members
remain in the public service long enough to know any men's
qualities intimately.  The leaders the Senate prefers are
almost of necessity its most conservative men, — men most
likely to magnify the powers and prerogatives of the body
they represent and to stickle for every privilege it possesses, not at all likely to look to the President for leadership or to yield to the House upon any radical difference
of opinion or of purpose.

Particularly in its dealings with the President has the
Senate shown its pride of independence, its desire to rule
rather than to be merely consulted, its inclination to magnify its powers and in some sense preside over the policy of
the government.  There can be little doubt in the mind of
any one who has carefully studied the plans and opinions
of the Constitutional Convention of 1787 that the relations
of the President and Senate were intended to be very much
more intimate and confidential than they have been; that
it was expected that the Senate would give the President
its advice and consent in respect of appointments and
treaties in the spirit of an executive council associated
with him upon terms of confidential coöperation rather
than in the spirit of an independent branch of the government, jealous lest he should in the least particular attempt
to govern its judgment or infringe upon its prerogatives.
The formality and stiffness, the attitude as if of rivalry and
mutual distrust, which have marked the dealings of the
President with the Senate, have shown a tendency to increase rather than to decrease as the years have gone by,

and have undoubtedly at times very seriously embarrassed the action of the government in many difficult and important matters.

The Senate has shown itself particularly stiff and jealous in insisting upon exercising an independent judgment upon foreign affairs, and has done so so often that a sort of customary *modus vivendi* has grown up between the President and the Senate, as of rival powers. The Senate is expected in most instances to accept the President's appointments to office, and the President is expected to be very tolerant of the Senate's rejection of treaties, proposing but by no means disposing even in this chief field of his power. Advisers who are entirely independent of the official advised are in a position to be, not his advisers, but his masters; and when, as sometimes happens, the Senate is of one political party and the President of the other, its dictation may be based, not upon the merits of the question involved, but upon party antagonisms and calculations of advantage.

The President has not the same recourse when blocked by the Senate that he has when opposed by the House. When the House declines his counsel he may appeal to the nation, and if public opinion respond to his appeal the House may grow thoughtful of the next congressional elections and yield; but the Senate is not so immediately sensitive to opinion and is apt to grow, if anything, more stiff if pressure of that kind is brought to bear upon it.

But there is another course which the President may follow, and which one or two Presidents of unusual political sagacity have followed, with the satisfactory results that were to have been expected. He may himself be less stiff and offish, may himself act in the true spirit of the Constitution and establish intimate relations of confidence with the Senate on his own initiative, not carrying his plans to completion and then laying them in final form before the Senate to be accepted or rejected, but keeping himself in confidential communication with the leaders of the Senate while his plans are in course, when their advice will be of service to him and his information of the greatest service to them, in order that there may be veritable counsel and a real accommodation of views instead of a final challenge and contest. The policy which has made rivals of the President and Senate has shown itself in the President as often as in the Senate, and if the Constitution did indeed intend that the Senate should in such matters be an executive council it is not only the privilege of the President to treat it as such, it is also his best policy and his plain duty. As it is now, the President and Senate are apt to deal with each other with the formality and punctilio of powers united by no common tie except the vague common tie of public interest, but it is within their choice to change the whole temper of affairs in such matters and to exhibit the true spirit of the Constitution by coming into intimate relations of mutual confidence, by a change of attitude which can perhaps be effected more easily upon the initiative of the President than upon the initiative of the Senate.

It is manifestly the duty of statesmen, with whatever branch of the government they may be associated, to study in a very serious spirit of public service the right accommodation of parts in this complex system of ours, the accommodation which will give the government its best force and synthesis in the face of the difficult counsels and perplexing tasks of regulation with which it is face to face, and no one can play the leading part in such a matter with more influence or propriety than the President. If he have character, modesty, devotion, and insight as well as force, he can bring the contending elements of the system together into a great and efficient body of common counsel.

# VI

## THE COURTS

OUR courts are the balance-wheel of our whole constitutional system; and ours is the only constitutional system so balanced and controlled. Other constitutional systems lack complete poise and certainty of operation because they lack the support and interpretation of authoritative, undisputable courts of law. It is clear beyond all need of exposition that for the definite maintenance of constitutional understandings it is indispensable, alike for the preservation of the liberty of the individual and for the preservation of the integrity of the powers of the government, that there should be some non-political forum in which those understandings can be impartially debated and determined. That forum our courts supply. There the individual may assert his rights; there the government must accept definition of its authority. There the individual may challenge the legality of governmental action and have it judged by the test of fundamental principles, and that test the government must abide; there the government can check the too aggressive self-assertion of the individual and establish its power upon lines which all can comprehend and heed. The constitutional powers of the courts constitute the ultimate safeguard alike of individual privilege and of governmental prerogative. It is in this sense that our judiciary is the balance-wheel

142

of our entire system; it is meant to maintain that nice adjustment between individual rights and governmental powers which constitutes political liberty.

I am not now thinking of the courts as the lawyer thinks of them, as places of technical definition and business adjustment, where the rights of individuals as against one another are debated and determined; but as the citizen thinks of them, as his safeguard against a too arrogant and teasing use of power by the government, an instrument of politics, — of liberty. Constitutional government exists in its completeness and full reality only when the individual, only when every individual, is regarded as a partner of the government in the conduct of the nation's life. The citizen is not individually represented in any assembly or in any regularly constituted part of the government itself. He cannot, except in the most extraordinary cases and with the utmost difficulty, bring his individual private affairs to the attention of Congress or of his state legislature, to the attention of the President of the United States or of the executive officer of his state; he would find himself balked of relief if he did by the laws under which they act and exercise their clearly specified powers. It is only in the courts that men are individuals in respect of their rights. Only in them can the individual citizen set up his private right and interest against the government by an appeal to the fundamental understandings upon which the government rests. In no other government but our own can he set them up even there against the government. He can everywhere set them up against other individuals who would invade his rights or who have imposed upon him, but not against the government. The government under every other constitutional system but our own is sovereign, unquestionable, to be restrained not by the courts but only by public opinion, only by the opinion of the nation acting through the representative chamber. We alone have given our courts power to restrain the government under which they themselves act and from which they themselves derive their authority.

And this is not merely because our constitutional understandings are explicitly set forth in written documents which the courts must regard as part of the body of law they are charged to maintain and interpret, — the chief and fundamental part to which all other parts must give way; for a very important part of the constitutional understandings upon which the English government rests is written in Magna Carta and in the great Bill of Rights, and yet the English courts have no authority to check the law-making organs of the government even though they override Magna Carta and the Bill of Rights in the statutes which they enact. No doubt the definitions of Magna Carta and of the Bill of Rights lie at the foundation of all government and of all individual privilege in England, and if any statute of doubtful interpretation were brought before an English court which seemed in contravention of rights clearly stated in those documents, the court would interpret it in accordance with the terms of those revered instruments of liberty; but if a statute should in plain terms ignore the definitions and restrictions even of Magna Carta and the Bill of Rights, I understand that the court would be obliged to enforce it. Parliament is sovereign and can do what it pleases. Only the opinion of the nation can check or restrain it. Only repeal can set an obnoxious statute aside. No government is more entirely governed by opinion than the government of England, but it is gov-

erned by the general opinion of the nation, not by the
particular opinion of the courts.

This is not because the English courts have been less interested than our own to maintain individual rights and
liberties or less liberal in their interpretation of individual
privilege. No courts have been more liberal or more disposed to safeguard private privilege. The common law of
England has, more than any other law, been a mirror of
opinion and of social adjustment and has been made in
its development to fit English life like a well-cut garment.
Time out of mind English judges have liberalized and
broadened it by reading into it good principle and enlightened opinion. There are some notable old cases in
the English law reports in which the judges declare all
principles of right reason and of humanity to be parts of
the common law of England without precedent. But
there is no fundamental law susceptible of interpretation
by the courts which defines or limits the powers of Parliament. Magna Carta and the Bill of Rights define the
rights of individuals as against the crown, but not as against
Parliament, not as against those whom the nation has
authorized to make its laws. Upon them no document
which the courts can read or elucidate as law places any
restraint. The courts must enforce whatever they enact.
The powers of our law-making bodies are, on the contrary, very definitely defined and circumscribed in documents which are themselves part of the body of our law,
and the decisions of the courts interpreting those documents set those law-making bodies their limits.

To us this power of the courts seems natural not only
but of the essence of the whole system; but it is in fact
extraordinary and has been looked upon by not a few of

our foreign critics with unaffected amazement. And they have been the more amazed because they did not find this extraordinary power conferred upon our courts in any part or sentence of our fundamental law. "The judicial power of the United States," so run the quiet sentences of the Constitution, "shall be vested in one supreme Court and in such inferior Courts as the Congress may from time to time ordain and establish" and "shall extend to all Cases in Law and Equity arising under this Constitution, the Laws of the United States, and Treaties made or which shall be made under their Authority." It is only an inference drawn by the courts themselves that "the laws of the United States and treaties made under their authority" shall be tested by the Constitution and disallowed if they lie outside the field of power it has granted Congress and the President, — a very plain inference, no doubt, but only an inference: an inference made upon analogy, drawn out of historical circumstances and out of a definite theory as to the origin of our government.

There was never any sovereign government in America. The governments of the colonies were operated under charters granted by the English crown, and could legally exercise no powers which those charters did not confer. If they exceeded those powers, the king could annul their acts, and the king's courts could declare their charters forfeited. The same principle and practice still obtains with regard to the powers of the chartered English colonies. The constitution of Canada is "the British North America Act," an act of Parliament, federating the several provinces, giving each its legislature and its separate field of law, and setting over all the Governor and Parliament of the Dominion. Anything done either by the government of the provinces or by the government of the Dominion in excess or contravention of the terms of the British North America Act is null and void and can be so treated by the courts of the Dominion itself, though an appeal lies in all cases of such consequence to the Judicial Committee of the Privy Council in England, a court of the sovereign power. The sovereign power now set over us is the people. When the authority of the crown lapsed by revolution, they assumed it. For colonial charters they substituted their state constitutions, to which they presently added the Constitution of the United States. Their sovereign grant of power can no more be exceeded than can the grants of the sovereign king of the older day or the sovereign Parliament of our own time. Statutes must conform to the Constitution and are null and void if they do not. Our constitutions are comparable, say Professor Dicey and Mr. Bryce, to the charters of great corporations, our statutes to their by-laws, our treaties to their contracts. No by-law or contract made by them will be upheld by any court if in contravention or excess of their charter powers. Any English-speaking lawyer would have reasoned the matter out as we have reasoned it out.

None the less, plain inference though it be, this power of our courts renders our constitutional system unique. No other constitutional system has this balance and means of energy, — this means of energy for the individual citizen. The individual citizen among us can apply the checks of law to the government upon his own initiative, and they will respond to his touch as readily as to the touch of the greatest political officer of the system. More readily, indeed, for the courts will not hear abstract questions. Some concrete and tangible interest, involving the right of some particular individual or corporation, must be implicated, and implicated in some form which makes a legal inquiry and remedy both necessary and possible under the ordinary rules of suit and procedure. They will not take the question up otherwise, and an individual citizen is a more natural and usual party to such an inquiry than an officer of the government. An officer of the government cannot be a party to a suit in his official capacity except as he represents some claim or defense of the government itself. The rights of the individual touch the subject-matter of the law at a thousand points, and he may in mere controversy with his neighbor call in question rights which his neighbor professes to exercise under the authority of acts of Congress. No officer of the government need be or can be a party to such a suit; the court is adjudicating private rights and will not hesitate to set an act of Congress aside if it invade those rights in contravention or in excess of the powers granted Congress in the Constitution.

Only by slow and searching labor have the courts been able to keep our singularly complex system at its right poise and adjustment. It has required a long line of cases to thread its intricacies and afford the individual a complete administration of its safeguards. It is a system of many counterpoises and prescriptions. First, there are the restrictions placed upon our governments in respect of the powers they can use upon the individual. Congress can exercise no powers except those explicitly or by plain implication conferred upon it by the Constitution. And there are certain things which it is explicitly forbidden to do. "The privilege of a writ of Habeas Corpus shall not be suspended, unless when in Cases of Rebellion or Invasion public safety may require it. No Bill of Attainder or *ex post facto* Law shall be passed." The powers not granted to Congress remain with the states, but certain powers are denied the states by their own constitutions, some by the Constitution of the United States. "No State shall enter into any Treaty, Alliance, or Federation; grant Laws of Marque or Reprisal; coin money; emit Bills of Credit; make any Thing but gold and silver Coin a Tender in Payment of Debts; pass any Bill of Attainder, *ex post facto* Law or Law impairing the Obligation of Contracts, or grant any Title of Nobility," is the language of Section X of the first article of the Constitution. And added to the restrictions placed upon state and federal governments by the Constitution of the United States are the still more complex and numerous limitations imposed upon the states by their own constitutions. All these, from whatever constitution drawn, the courts must interpret and enforce. In respect of all of them the courts are instruments for the protection of the individual. Besides these definitions and restrictions, which partake of the nature of a Bill of Rights, our constitutions apportion power between the states and the federal government, and that apportionment the courts must assist to make definite and secure. They apportion powers also to the several parts of our state and federal governments, the executive, the legislature, and the courts themselves, and this apportionment also the courts must define and maintain.

It is thus that they are the balance-wheel of the whole system, taking the strain from every direction and seeking to maintain what any unchecked exercise of power might destroy. They are at once instruments of the individual against the government, of the government against the individual, of the several members of our political union against one another, and of the several parts of government in their legal synthesis and adjustment. No wonder De Tocqueville marveled at the "variety of information and excellence of discretion" expected of the American citizen by the constitutional system under which he lives. All these things he may sooner or later find himself obliged to call upon the courts to adjudicate and keep at their right balance for his sake, that the terms of his partnership with the government may be strictly and righteously observed.

It throws upon him a great responsibility and expects of him a constant and watchful independence. There is no one to look out for his rights but himself. He is not a ward of the government, but his own guardian. The law is not automatic; he must himself put it into operation, and he must show good cause why the courts should exert the great powers vested in them. They will not allow the validity of any statute or treaty or of any act of the government to be called lightly in question or drawn unnecessarily under discussion. He must show that, in order to determine definite, concrete rights of his own which are in dispute between himself and his opponent in litigation, it is necessary that the courts should answer the question he raises as to the validity of what the government has done or attempted; not drawing them on to an abstract thesis, but bringing them face to face with an actual question of law. If it lies in his direct way to do that, it makes no difference in what court he raises the question. It need not be the Supreme Court of the United States or the highest court of the state in which he brings suit. Any court can adjudicate the question of the constitutionality of the acts of the government, if it have jurisdiction over the general subject-matter of the case in which the question is raised. The dignity of the question does not alter the jurisdiction. Of course, constitutional questions of capital importance are very likely to be carried sooner or later to the Supreme Court by processes of appeal, but they may originate in any court of any grade and belong not to the extraordinary but to the ordinary processes of adjudication. It may fall in the way of any court in the ordinary administration of justice to compare by-laws with charters, statutes with constitutions, the subordinate parts of the law with the ultimate and fundamental parts, the acts of the government with their legal norms and standards.

The same jurisdiction would no doubt spring up in England were the rules of the British constitution to be reduced to writing and put upon the footing of Magna Carta, were the authority of Parliament to be limited and defined by charter as the authority of the crown has time out of mind been. For English legal practice is the same as American. American practice was derived from it. In England, as in America, the individual citizen is bidden take care of himself, not only against his neighbor but also, if he can, against the government. In England, as in America, an officer of the law ceases to be an officer of the law when he acts in excess of his authority. He may be fined or imprisoned or executed as any other man would be if he overstep the limits of his warrant and authority and do things which he has no right to do. He has no authority but that which is legal and for which he can show rightful warrant. But it is not so in any other country. In every other country an officer of the government is an officer whatever he may do, and cannot be haled before the ordinary courts. He will be restrained from doing illegal things, but only by his superiors, to whom injured persons must complain, or by special administrative tribunals provided for the purpose, before which the individual may cite him. No superior officer, no administrative court, will handle a complaint against him as an ordinary court would handle a suit or indictment. The offense charged will be looked at from the point of view of administrative officers, as a public indiscretion rather than as a private wrong; great latitude will be allowed an officer of the law if he profess to act in the public interest and cannot be shown to have acted in malice. The atmosphere of the inquiry is the atmosphere of authority, and the discipline applied will be the discipline of a corps, not the judgment of an ordinary court against a breaker of the law. Citizens are subjects, not partners of the government. It is against the whole spirit of our polity, on the contrary, that we should be running to the government with complaints. Our practice is built upon individual rights, and the individual is freely given the means to take care of himself in courts which are his own no less than they are the government's. The courts are meant to be the people's forum, open to all who wish the law determined.

It is of the deeper consequence that the courts should in fact be open to all, equally accessible and serviceable to every man. If it be true, as it is nowadays common to charge, that our courts are serviceable only to the rich, we should look to it, for in that case our system is impaired at its very heart; its poise and balance are gone. *Are* our courts as available for the poor as for the rich? It is not a question of impartiality or fairness, of disposition to hear the suit of the poor as readily and as attentively as the suit of the rich. Some inferior men are no doubt appointed to our federal bench; our state courts are many of them filled by processes of election which take account of the judge's political opinions and of his service to a political party rather than of his learning or of his rank among his fellow practitioners at the bar, and many men are chosen who are not suitable either in character or attainments; but the average integrity of the American bench is extraordinarily high. There are not many courts of which it can justly be said that a man will be denied his legal rights because he is poor or without influential connections. The question I raise is of another kind. Are not poor men in fact excluded from our courts by the cost and the length of their processes? The rich man can afford the cost of litigation; what is of more consequence, he can afford the delays of trial and appeal; he has a margin of resources which makes it possible for him to wait the months, it may be the years, during which the process of adjudication will drag on and during which the rights he is contesting will be suspended, the interests involved tied up. But the poor man can afford neither the one nor the other. He might afford the initial expense, if he could be secure against delays; but delays he cannot abide without ruin. I fear that it must be admitted that our present processes of adjudication lack both simplicity and promptness, that they are unnecessarily expensive, and that a rich litigant can almost always tire a poor one out and readily cheat him of his rights by simply leading him through an endless maze of appeals and technical delays.

If this be true, our very constitutional principle has

fallen into dangerous disrepair, and our immediate duty is to amend and simplify our processes of justice. There is no guarantee of liberty under a system like ours, if the courts be not as accessible and as serviceable to the poor man as to the rich. Of course, they never can be so literally. The processes of justice must always, if they are to be thorough, be deliberate, not hurried, often elaborate, not always simple. Even if they were available to the poor man without any cost whatever in money, they must in any case cost him something in time and trouble; and the very poor, tied to their tasks in fear of momentary need, cannot spend time or attention on anything which does not earn them bread. But it were shame upon us if we could not bring our courts nearer to the poor man than they are now, and the most immediately necessary reform of our system lies in that direction. The individual of whatever grade or character must be afforded opportunity to take care of himself, whether against the power of his neighbor or against the power of the government.

I have spoken of the state and federal courts without discrimination. They are all branches of the people's forum. Constitutional questions may be determined by them all, of whatever grade, because individual rights must be adjudicated by them all. But it is interesting to observe the line that runs between state and federal jurisdictions. It affords a sort of insight into the character of our complex constitutional system which no other part of our study can afford. The political relations between the states and the federal government I shall consider in another lecture, and inasmuch as their political relations rest in large measure in a system like ours upon their legal relations, I will reserve also the greater part of what I have to say about the law of their union and separation until all parts of the picture may be put together in a single sketch. But some part of the matter lies immediately under our eyes here.

The tests of the federal Constitution can be applied in the state courts, and the tests of the state constitutions in the federal courts, but only in such a way as to make the federal courts the final judges of what the meaning and intent of the federal Constitution is, and the state courts the final judges and interpreters of what the state constitutions forbid or require. The Constitution of the United States makes the federal courts the forum for the trial, not only of cases arising under federal law, but also for the trial of suits between litigants who are citizens of different states and who have therefore no other common tribunal. Cases between citizens of different states need not be tried in the courts of the United States, if the litigants are content to submit them to the courts of the state in which the cause of action arose; but the federal courts are open to them; and if in such a case tried in them it should become necessary to interpret the provisions of a state constitution, the federal courts must of course attempt that interpretation as they would attempt any other question the case might bring under their examination. But they would feel themselves obliged to adopt the interpretation already put upon those provisions by the courts of the state whose constitution was under examination. Only when there were no decisions of the courts of the state upon the subject would they feel at liberty to follow their own reading and interpretation. The courts of the United States have not the right to impose upon litigants their own interpretations of the fundamental law of a state when that law in no way involves the jurisdiction or the authority of the federal government, and in the trial of ordinary cases between citizens of different states they must hold themselves to the administration of state laws as they are interpreted by the courts of the states in which they originated.

Similarly, the courts of the states are at liberty to determine cases which involve an interpretation of the Constitution of the United States. No question is foreign to them which belongs to a case regularly instituted before them; but they in their turn are bound to follow in such matters the decisions of the courts of the United States, so far as they may have covered the matter drawn in question. The courts of the United States must be the ultimate judges of the meaning and intent of federal law, as the courts of the states are of the principles of state law. A litigant in a state court may contend, for example, that some statute, or even some constitutional provision, of the state, under which his opponent is suing him or making defense, is inconsistent with the Constitution of the United States. If the court uphold him in this contention and treat the law which he challenges as null and void because inconsistent with federal law, there is an end of the matter. The court has upheld federal law against the law of the state, and no appeal can be taken to a court of the United States, — which could do no more. But if the court disallow the plea and declare the state law valid notwithstanding its alleged conflict with the law of the United States, the defeated litigant may take an appeal to the courts of the United States; for with a federal tribunal must lie the final determination of the conflict, lest the state court might have been biased in favor of the law and privilege of the state under whose authority it acted.

The significance of this principle of action is that the federal government is, through its courts, in effect made the final judge of its own powers. In no case can a conflict of authority between it and the government of a state be finally decided against it by a state court, by any court but its own, if the parties in interest choose to appeal. The whole balance of our federal system, therefore, lies in the federal courts. It is inevitable that it should be so. Our constitutional law could have no final certainty otherwise. "This Constitution, and the Laws of the United States which are made in Pursuance thereof; and all Treaties made, or which shall be made, under the authority of the United States shall be the supreme Law of the Land; and the Judges in every State shall be bound thereby, any Thing in the Constitution or Laws of any State to the Contrary notwithstanding:" such is the definite, uncompromising language of the Constitution of the United States. No one can doubt that it was necessary for the maintenance of the system that the courts of the federal government should be the arbiters of all questions of disputed jurisdiction or conflicting authority. But of course such a principle constitutes the courts of the United States the guardians of our whole legal development. With them must lie the final statesmanship of control.

For by according such powers to our courts we virtually vest in them the statesmanship of control. The Constitution is not a mere lawyers' document: it is, as I have more than once said, the vehicle of a nation's life. No lawyer can read into a document anything subsequent to its execution; but we have read into the Constitution of the United States the whole expansion and transformation of our national life that has followed its adoption. We can say without the least disparagement or even criticism of the Supreme Court of the United States that at its hands the Constitution has received an adaptation and an elaboration which would fill its framers of the simple days of 1787 with nothing less than amazement. The explicitly granted powers of the Constitution are what they always were; but the powers drawn from it by implication have grown and multiplied beyond all expectation, and each generation of statesmen looks to the Supreme Court to supply the interpretation which will serve the needs of the day. It is a process necessary but full of peril. It is easier to form programs than to exercise a wise and moderate control, and the task of the courts calls for more poise, nicer discriminations of conscience, a steadier view of affairs, and a better knowledge of the principles of right action, than the task of Congress or of the President. Both the safety and the purity of our system depend on the wisdom and the good conscience of the Supreme Court. Expanded and adapted by interpretation the powers granted in the Constitution must be; but the manner and the motive of their expansion involve the integrity, and therefore the permanence, of our entire system of government.

By common consent the most notable and one of the most statesmanlike figures in our whole judicial history is the figure of John Marshall. No other name is comparable with his in fame or honor in this singular field of statesmanlike judicial control, — a field of our own marking out and creation, a statesmanship peculiar to our own annals. Marshall may be said to have created for us the principles of interpretation which have governed our national development. He created them like a great lawyer, master of the fundamental conceptions which have enlightened all great lawyers in the administration of law and have made it seem in their hands a system of life, not a mere body of technical rules; he created them also like a great statesman who sees his way as clearly without precedent as with it to those renderings of charter and statute which will vivify their spirit and enlarge their letter without straining a single tissue of the vital stuff of which they are made.

A thoughtful English judge has distinguished between those extensions of the meaning of law by interpretation which are the product of insight and conceived in the spirit of the law itself, and those which are the product of sheer will, of the mere determination that the law shall mean what it is convenient to have it mean. Marshall's interpretations were the products of insight. His learning was the learning of the seer, saturated with the spirit of the law, instinct with its principle of growth. No other method, no other principle has legitimate place in a system which depends for its very life upon its integrity, upon the candor and good conscience of its processes, upon keeping faith with its standards and its immemorial promises.

One of the most dramatic and interesting scenes in our history, the scene with which the imagination of the historian who is keenly alive to those processes of constitutional development which have made the nation and yet have threatened to unmake it is most engaged, is that enacted on the fourth of March, 1829, when Andrew Jackson, the sincere apostle of principles of action which were apt to make light of law, was sworn into office by John Marshall, the aged Chief Justice at whose hands the law of the nation had received alike its majesty and its liberal spirit of ordered progress. Jackson himself was not young. He had grown gray in having his own way, in acting upon principles he deemed right, whether they had the warrant of law or not; — no outlaw; on the contrary, a man of conscience and honor, but habituated to the principles of the frontier and of the field of battle, where action did not wait upon law but formed itself on the exigencies of the occasion. He took the oath of office in all solemnity and good faith, swearing "to the best of his ability to preserve, protect, and defend the Constitution of the United States." But he afterward explained, when he chose to ignore the decisions of the Supreme Court, uttered by Chief Justice Marshall in authoritative interpretation of the Constitution, that he had sworn to uphold and preserve it as he understood it, and would take no dictation as to its meaning from any source but his own intelligence and conscience. The two men were at the antipodes from one another both in principle and in character; had no common insight into the institutions of the country which they served; represented one the statesmanship of will and the other the statesmanship of control. General Jackson was a brave man, devoted to the performance of his duty with a genuine ardor of unselfish patriotism, and rendered services in his administration of the great office he held for which he must always be honored so long as the large interests of the nation are understood; but he was the sort of man who might very easily twist and destroy our whole constitutional system, were the courts robbed of their authority and the great balance-wheel of their power shaken from its gearings. One might moralize upon the picture of these two old men standing there face to face at Jackson's inauguration until he had expounded the very genius of our institutions. Marshall, putting the

oath of office to Jackson, was repeating in quiet, modern
form the transaction of Runnymede.

Some German critics of our constitutional system,
trained in another school of politics and another school of
law, have looked upon the powers of our courts as a dangerous anomaly. We have, they say, taken our courts out
of their proper sphere and put them where courts do
not belong, in the field of politics, where they are set as
masters over Congress and the President by whom the
policies of the nation are formed. But such criticisms
ignore both the principle of constitutional government and
the actual practice of our courts. They emanate from
men for whom all law is the voice of government and who
regard the government as the source of all law, who cannot conceive of a law set above government and to which
it must conform. It must be admitted that such a law
is not everywhere essential to the maintenance of constitutional government. The English nation restrains its
king by written compact, but it has never restrained its
Parliament. Parliament its law leaves supreme because
Parliament is representative of the nation, and opinion
is strong and concerted enough to restrain it without law
and the assistance of the courts. But we faced a very
singular task when we undertook to combine the one-time
colonies of England in America into a constitutional federal state. There had been no time to form a national
habit or accumulate precedents with regard to a common
government. It was necessary to create it by law, to
accommodate its various parts to one another by law, to
define both its powers and the relations of the people to it
by law. No other constitutional understanding was ever
quite so detailed or so definite, no other constitutional

M

understanding ever rested upon just such foundations of circumstance and purpose.

But we did not, with all our inventing, create anything abnormal or unnatural; and our continental critics mistake the actual practice of our courts in acting upon constitutional questions. They do not act as instruments of politics, but only as modest instruments of law, as any other courts would. A very superficial examination of the constitutional decisions of the Supreme Court of the United States will suffice to show how careful it has been to refrain from even the appearance of dictating to Congress or to the executive. It has sought to respect their authority and to give full scope to their discretion in every possible way, at every possible point, never setting its judgment or opinion against theirs in any case which admitted of reasonable doubt, never drawing political questions into discussion, but confining itself most scrupulously to its proper business of adjudicating individual rights, whether those rights arise under the Constitution or under statutes; and it has demanded that a very clear case be made out against any act of Congress said by the litigants before it to be unconstitutional, before it would venture to set aside what Congress had ordained. In no instance has it acted upon political grounds when setting aside an act of Congress, but always upon clearly defined legal grounds, because the act had been shown to be inconsistent with indisputable provisions of the fundamental charter of the government itself. There could be no alternative in the case of a government of limited and specified powers.

And there has never been any serious friction between Congress and the courts. Occasional irritation there has been, of course. Congressmen have sometimes, forgetting their constitutional principles, spoken in sharp and resentful criticism of the presumption of federal judges who have declared favorite pieces of legislation unconstitutional and refused to execute statutes by means of which politicians had hoped to store up credit to themselves or their party. Senators have shown a particular sensitiveness in the matter. There are many distinguished lawyers in the Senate whose opinion upon points of law ought no doubt to be regarded as individually quite as weighty and conclusive as that of a district or circuit judge of the United States who has declined to enforce acts which had passed under their scrutiny. Second-class lawyers, it has been said in heat, men who had themselves once been members of the House or Senate and who had there shown their inferiority in legal discussion, venture, when appointed to seats on the bench, to set aside the judgments of the very men who formerly worsted them in debate upon those very questions. But members of Congress must usually be patient under these crosses. They will often remember that it was upon their own recommendation that these very men, their one-time comrades, were appointed by the President; that the appointments passed the scrutiny of the Judiciary Committee of the Senate and were confirmed; and that the point of view of the lawyer in Congress is after all not always the point of view of the lawyer on the bench, whose concern is not with political considerations, but with the legal rights of the litigants before him and the exact maintenance of the terms of the law.

There are instances which they will recall which are full of instruction. Mr. Salmon P. Chase, when Secretary of the Treasury under Mr. Lincoln, advocated the issue of irredeemable paper currency in relief of the Treasury, and was largely instrumental in inducing Congress to pass the statutes which filled the country with "greenbacks," declaring it to be his opinion that such issues were legal under the powers granted Congress in the Constitution; but Mr. Salmon P. Chase, when afterward Chief Justice of the United States, joined with the majority of that great court in declaring the legal tender acts unconstitutional. The thing might happen with the most conscientious lawyer. It is one thing to have to decide a matter of that kind in connection with important business you are conducting, and it is quite another thing to have it to decide as a judge lifted above all personal interest in the matter and bidden take it upon its merits, not as an advocate but as an arbiter.

Undoubtedly federal judges may be mistaken and lawyers in Congress right, if the lawyers in Congress be of better stuff morally and intellectually than the judges they have recommended or allowed the President to appoint; but that simply points an old moral. No part of any government is any better than the men who administer it. A distinguished member of a well-known reform club once told me that after twenty years of hard work in trying to further the objects of good government to which the club had devoted itself, he had a very humiliating confession to make. Throughout all those years he had labored assiduously to get the laws of the State in which he lived modified and improved, and to have all practices of which his club disapproved in state or city governments made illegal by statute. Year after year he had gone to the capital of the state and pressed every legitimate influence he could command to induce the legislature to enact the desired laws, and once and again he had succeeded. But government did not seem to be reformed, whatever his success. Old practices went on unchecked, or took new forms, or eluded the processes of law. It was a long lesson, and he had very stubbornly refused to learn it, but he had learned it at last and was now ready to make his confession that after all he had been mistaken: the way to reform government was to elect good men to conduct it, and that was the whole matter. Good laws were desirable, but good men were indispensable, and could make even bad laws yield pure and righteous government.

Every government is a government of men, not of laws, and of course the courts of the United States are no wiser or better than the judges who constitute them. A series of bad appointments might easily make them inferior to every other branch of the government in their comprehension of constitutional principles, their perception of constitutional values. But that would be because the government had fallen into wrong hands, and would not invalidate the principle upon which our courts are constituted and empowered. It is an argument for electing the right men to the presidency and to the Senate, which confirms the President's appointments; it is not an argument for changing our constitutional arrangements. The constitutional powers of the courts are no less indispensable, no less central and essential to our whole system and conception of government, because they are sometimes unwise or unintelligent in their exercise of them.

Indeed, it is not easy to speak of this subject, so fundamental, so deeply significant, without pausing to point out the interesting interdependence of the several parts of our government and the many contingencies upon which their excellence and their integrity depend. The courts of the United States control the action of the other branches of the government in the interest of our fundamental constitutional understandings; and yet the courts of the United States are constituted by federal statute and by the President's appointment. The judicial power of the United States is vested "in one Supreme Court and in such inferior courts as Congress may from time to time ordain and establish"; only the Supreme Court exists by direct provision of the Constitution itself. Other courts Congress may establish or abolish, increase or decrease, assign to this jurisdiction or to that. The Constitution provides, indeed, that all judges of the United States shall hold their offices during good behavior, but Congress could readily overcome a hostile majority in any court or in any set of courts, even in the Supreme Court itself, by a sufficient increase in the number of judges and an adroit manipulation of jurisdictions, and could with the assistance of the President make them up to suit its own purposes. These two "coördinate" branches of the government, to which the courts speak in such authoritative fashion with regard to the powers they may and may not exercise under the Constitution, — namely, Congress and the executive, — may, in fact, if they choose, manipulate the courts to their own ends without formal violation of any provision of the fundamental law of the land. There has never been any serious fear that they would do anything of the kind, though an occasional appointment to the Supreme Court has made the country suspicious and uneasy. But it is well to keep the matter clearly before us, if only that we may remind ourselves of the only absolute safeguards of a constitutional system. They lie in the character, the independence, the resolution, the right purpose of the men who vote and who choose the public servants of whom the government is to consist. Any government can be corrupted, any government may fall into disrepair. It consists of men, and the men of whom it consists will be no better than the men who choose them. The courts are the people's forum; they are also the index of the government's and of the nation's character.

The weightiest import of the matter is seen only when it is remembered that the courts are the instruments of the nation's growth, and that the way in which they serve that use will have much to do with the integrity of every national process. If they determine what powers are to be exercised under the Constitution, they by the same token determine also the adequacy of the Constitution in respect of the needs and interests of the nation; our conscience in matters of law and our opportunity in matters of politics are in their hands. There is so much to justify the criticism of our German critics; but they have not put their fingers upon the right point of criticism. It is not true that in judging of what Congress or the President has done, our courts enter the natural field of discretion or of judgment which belongs to other branches of government, — a field in its nature political, where lie the choices of policy and of authority. That field they respectfully avoid, and confine themselves to the necessary conclusions drawn from written law. But it is true that their power is political; that if they had interpreted the Constitution in its strict letter, as some proposed, and not in its spirit, like the charter of a business corporation and not like the charter of a living government, the vehicle of a nation's life, it would have proved a strait-jacket, a means not of liberty and development, but of mere restriction and embarrassment. I have spoken of the statesmanship of control expected of our courts; but there is also the statesmanship of adaptation characteristic of all great systems of law since the days of the Roman prætor; and there can be no doubt that we have been singular among the nations in looking to our courts for that double function of statesmanship, for the means of growth as well as for the restraint of ordered method.

But our courts have stood the test, chiefly because John Marshall presided over their processes during the formative period of our national life. He was of the school and temper of Washington. He read constitutions in search of their spirit and purpose and understood them in the light of the conceptions under the influence of which they were framed. He saw in them not mere negations of power, but grants of power, and he reasoned from out the large political experience of the race as to what those grants meant, what they were intended to accomplish, not as a pedant but as a statesman, rather; and every generation of statesmen since his day have recognized the fact that it was he more than the men in Congress or in the President's chair who gave to our federal government its scope and power. The greatest statesmen are always those who attempt their tasks with imagination, with a large vision of things to come, but with the conscience of the lawyer, also, the knowledge that law must be built, not wrested, to their use and purpose. And so, whether by force of circumstance or by deliberate design, we have married legislation with adjudication and look for statesmanship in our courts.

No one can truly say that our courts have held us back

or have ever exhibited a spirit of mere literalness and reaction. Many a series of cases has built the implications of the Constitution out to meet the needs and the changing circumstances of the nation's life. The process has seemed at times a little too facile. The courts have seemed upon occasion to seek in the law what they wished to find rather than what frank and legitimate inference would yield. Once and again they have been all too complacent in giving Congress leave to read its powers as best suited its convenience at a particular exigency in affairs. It is to be feared that they did so in connection with the many difficult questions which arose in regard to the settlements which followed upon the war between the states. But for the most part their method and their inferences have been conservative enough. The wonder is that they have kept so level a keel while serving a nation which has always insisted upon carrying so much sail.

When the Constitution was framed there were no railways, there was no telegraph, there was no telephone. The Supreme Court has read the power of Congress to establish post-offices and post-roads and to regulate commerce with foreign nations and among the several states to mean that it has jurisdiction over practically every matter connected with intercourse between the states. Railways are highways; telegraph and telephone lines are new forms of the post. The Constitution was not meant to hold the government back to the time of horses and wagons, the time when postboys carried every communication that passed from merchant to merchant, when trade had few long routes within the nation and did not venture in bulk beyond neighborhood transactions. The United States have clearly from generation to generation been taking on more and more of the characteristics of a community; more and more have their economic interests come to seem common interests; and the courts have rightly endeavored to make the Constitution a suitable instrument of the national life, extending to the things that are now common the rules that it established for similar things that were common at the beginning.

The real difficulty has been to draw the line where this process of expansion and adaptation ceases to be legitimate and becomes a mere act of will on the part of the government, served by the courts. The temptation to overstep the proper boundaries has been particularly great in interpreting the meaning of the words, "commerce among the several states." Manifestly, in a commercial nation almost every item of life directly or indirectly affects commerce, and our commerce is almost all of it on the grand scale. There is a vast deal of buying and selling, of course, within the boundaries of each state, but even the buying and selling which is done within a single state constitutes in our day but a part of that great movement of merchandise along lines of railway and watercourse which runs without limit and without regard to political jurisdiction. State commerce seems almost impossible to distinguish from interstate commerce. It has all come to seem part of what Congress may unquestionably regulate, though the makers of the Constitution may never have dreamed of anything like it and the tremendous interests which it affects. Which part of the complex thing may Congress regulate?

Clearly, any part of the actual movement of merchandise and persons from state to state. May it also regulate the conditions under which the merchandise is produced

which is presently to become the subject-matter of interstate commerce? May it regulate the conditions of labor
in field and factory? Clearly not, I should say; and I
should think that any thoughtful lawyer who felt himself
at liberty to be frank would agree with me. For that
would be to destroy all lines of division between the field
of state legislation and the field of federal legislation.
Back of the conditions of labor in the field and in the
factory lie all the intimate matters of morals and of domestic and business relationship which have always been
recognized as the undisputed field of state law; and these
conditions that lie back of labor may easily be shown
to have their part in determining the character and efficiency of commerce between the states. If the federal
power does not end with the regulation of the actual movements of trade, it ends nowhere, and the line between
state and federal jurisdiction is obliterated. But this
is not universally seen or admitted. It is, therefore, one
of the things upon which the conscience of the nation
must make test of itself, to see if it still retain that spirit
of constitutional understanding which is the only ultimate
prop and support of constitutional government. It is
questions of this sort that show the true relation of our
courts to our national character and our system of government.

The relation of the courts to opinion is a difficult matter
to state, and as delicate as difficult; yet it lies directly in
our path. I have pointed out in previous lectures that
opinion was the great, indeed the only, coördinating force
in our system; that the only thing that gave the President
an opportunity to make good his leadership of his party
and of the nation as against the resistance or the indiffer-

ence of the House or Senate was his close and especial
relation to opinion the nation over, and that, without
some such leadership as opinion might sustain the President in exercising within the just limits of the law, our
system would be checked of all movement, deprived of all
practical synthesis by its complicated system of checks
and counterpoises. What relation, then, are the courts
to bear to opinion? The only answer that can be made
is this: judges of necessity belong to their own generation.
The atmosphere of opinion cannot be shut out of their
court rooms. Its influence penetrates everywhere in
every self-governed nation. What we should ask of our
judges is that they prove themselves such men as can discriminate between the opinion of the moment and the
opinion of the age, between the opinion which springs, a
legitimate essence, from the enlightened judgment of
men of thought and good conscience, and the opinion of
desire, of self-interest, of impulse and impatience. What
we should ask of ourselves is that we sustain the courts
in the maintenance of the true balance between law and
progress, and that we make it our desire to secure nothing
which cannot be secured by the just and thoughtful
processes which have made our system, so far, a model
before all the world of the reign of law.

# VII

THE question of the relation of the States to the federal government is the cardinal question of our constitutional system. At every turn of our national development we have been brought face to face with it, and no definition either of statesmen or of judges has ever quieted or decided it. It cannot, indeed, be settled by the opinion of any one generation, because it is a question of growth, and every successive stage of our political and economic development gives it a new aspect, makes it a new question. The general lines of definition which were to run between the powers granted to Congress and the powers reserved to the States the makers of the Constitution were able to draw with their characteristic foresight and lucidity; but the subject-matter of that definition is constantly changing, for it is the life of the nation itself. Our activities change alike their scope and their character with every generation. The old measures of the Constitution are every day to be filled with new grain as the varying crop of circumstances comes to maturity. It is clear enough that the general commercial interests, the general financial interests, the general economic interests of the country, were meant to be brought under the regulation of the federal government, which should act for all; and it is equally clear that what are the general commercial interests, what the general financial interests, what the general economic interests of the country, is a question of fact, to be determined by circumstances which change under our very eyes, and that, case by case, we are inevitably drawn on to include under the established definitions of the law matters new and unforeseen, which seem in their magnitude to give to the powers of Congress a sweep and vigor certainly never conceived possible by earlier generations of statesmen, sometimes almost revolutionary even in our own eyes. The subject-matter of this troublesome definition is the living body of affairs. To analyze it is to analyze the life of the nation.

It is difficult to discuss so critical and fundamental a question calmly and without party heat or bias when it has come once more, as it has now, to an acute stage. Just because it lies at the heart of our constitutional system to decide it wrongly is to alter the whole structure and operation of our government, for good or for evil, and one would wish never to see the passion of party touch it to distort it. A sobering sense of responsibility should fall upon every one who handles it. No man should argue it this way or that for party advantage. Desire to bring the impartial truth to light must, in such a case, be the first dictate alike of true statesmanship and of true patriotism. Every man should seek to think of it and to speak of it in the true spirit of the founders of the government and of all those who have spent their lives in the effort to confirm its just principles both in counsel and in action.

Almost every great internal crisis in our affairs has turned upon the question of state and federal rights. To take but two instances, it was the central subject-matter of the great controversy over tariff legislation which led to attempted nullification and of the still greater controversy over the extension of slavery which led to the war between the States; and those two controversies did more than any others in our history to determine the scope and character of the federal government.

The principle of the <u>division of powers between state and federal governments</u> is a very simple one when stated in its most general terms. It is that the legislatures of the States shall have control of all the general subject-matter of law, of private rights of every kind, of local interests, and of everything that directly concerns their people as communities, — free choice with regard to all matters of local regulation and development, and that Congress shall have control only of such matters as concern the peace and the commerce of the country as a whole. The opponents of the tariff of 1824 objected to the tariff system which Congress was so rapidly building up, that it went much beyond the simple and quite legitimate object of providing the federal government with revenue in such a way as to stimulate without too much disturbing the natural development of the industries of the country, and was unmistakably intended to guide and determine the whole trend of the nation's economic evolution, preferring the industries of one section of the country to those of another in its bestowal of protection and encouragement, and so depriving the States as self-governing communities of all free economic choice in the development of their resources. Congress persisted in its course; nullification failed as even so much as an effectual protest against the power of a government of which General Jackson was the head, — never so sure he was right as when he was opposed; and a critical matter, of lasting importance, was decided. The federal government was conceded the power to determine the economic opportunities of the States. It was suffered to become a general providence, to which each part of the country must look for its chance to make lucrative use of its material resources.

The slavery question, though it cut deeper into the social structure of a great section of the country and contained such heat as could not, when once given vent, be restrained from breaking into flame, as the tariff controversy had been, was, after all, a no more fundamental question, in its first essential form, than the question of the tariff. Could Congress exclude slavery from the territories of the United States and from newly formed States? If it could, manifestly the slavery system, once restricted in territory, would in time die of the strictures which bound it. Mr. Lincoln was quite right when he said that no nation could exist half slave and half free. But that was only by consequence. The immediate question was the power of Congress to determine the internal social and economic structure of society in the several States thereafter to be formed. It is not to my present purpose to trace the circumstances and influences which brought on the Civil War. The abolition of slavery by war, though natural, was not the necessary or logical *legal* consequence of the contention that Congress legitimately possessed the power which it had exercised in the constitution of the Northwest Territory and in the enactment of the Missouri Compromise. What happened before the momentous struggle was over came about by the mere logic of human nature, under stress of human passion. What concerns me in the present discussion is that here, again, as in the building up of a fostering tariff, what turned out to be a far-reaching change in the very conception of federal power had as its central point of controversy the question of the powers of the States as against the powers of the government at Washington. The whole spirit and action of the government were deeply altered in carrying that question one stage further towards a settlement.

And I am particularly interested to point out that here again, as in the tariff question, it was an inevitable controversy, springing, not out of theory, not out of the uneasy ambition of statesmen, but out of mere growth and imperious circumstance, out of the actual movement of affairs. Population was spreading over the great western areas of the country; new communities were forming, upon which lawyers could lay no binding prescriptions as to the life they should lead; new Territories were constantly to be organized, new States constantly to be admitted to the Union. A choice which every day assumed new forms was thrust upon Congress. Events gave it its variety, and Congress could not avoid the influences of opinion, which altered as circumstances changed, as it became more and more clear what the nation was to be. It was of the very stuff of daily business, forced upon Congress by the opinion of the country, to answer the inevitable question, What shall these new communities be allowed to do with themselves, what shall they be suffered to make of the nation? May Congress determine, or is it estopped by the reserved powers of the States? The choices of growth cannot be postponed, and they seem always to turn upon some definition of the powers of Congress, some new doubt as to where the powers of the States leave off and the powers of the federal government begin.

And now the question has come upon us anew. It is no longer sectional, but it is all the more subtle and intricate, all the less obvious and tangible in its elements, on that

N

account. It involves, first or last, the whole economic movement of the age, and necessitates an analysis which has not yet been even seriously attempted. Which parts of the many sided processes of the nation's economic development shall be left to the regulation of the States, which parts shall be given over to the regulation of the federal government? I do not propound this as a mere question of choice, a mere question of statesmanship, but also as a question, a very fundamental question, of constitutional law. What, reading our Constitution in its true spirit, neither sticking in its letter nor yet forcing it arbitrarily to mean what we wish it to mean, shall be the answer of our generation, pressed upon by gigantic economic problems the solution of which may involve not only the prosperity but also the very integrity of the nation, to the old question of the distribution of powers between Congress and the States? For us, as for previous generations, it is a deeply critical question. The very stuff of all our political principles, of all our political experience, is involved in it. In this all too indistinctly marked field of right choice our statesmanship shall achieve new triumphs or come to calamitous shipwreck.

The old theory of the sovereignty of the States, which used so to engage our passions, has lost its vitality. The war between the States established at least this principle, that the federal government is, through its courts, the final judge of its own powers. Since that stern arbitrament it would be idle, in any practical argument, to ask by what law of abstract principle the federal government is bound and restrained. Its power is "to regulate commerce between the States," and the attempts now made during every session of Congress to carry the implications of that power beyond the utmost boundaries of reasonable and honest inference show that the only limits likely to be observed by politicians are those set by the good sense and conservative temper of the country.

The proposed federal legislation with regard to the regulation of child labor affords a striking example. If the power to regulate commerce between the States can be stretched to include the regulation of labor in mills and factories, it can be made to embrace every particular of the industrial organization and action of the country. The only limitations Congress would observe, should the Supreme Court assent to such obviously absurd extravagancies of interpretation, would be the limitations of opinion and of circumstance.

It is important, therefore, to look at the facts and to understand the real character of the political and economic materials of our own day very clearly and with a statesmanlike vision, as the makers of the Constitution understood the conditions they dealt with. If the jealousies of the colonies and of the little States which sprang out of them had not obliged the makers of the Constitution to leave the greater part of legal regulation in the hands of the States, it would have been wise, it would even have been necessary, to invent such a division of powers as was actually agreed upon. It is not, at bottom, a question of sovereignty or of any other political abstraction; it is a question of vitality. Uniform regulation of the economic conditions of a vast territory and a various people like the United States would be mischievous, if not impossible. The statesmanship which really attempts it is premature and unwise. Undoubtedly the recent economic development of the country, particularly the development of the last two decades, has obliterated many boundaries, made many interests national and common, which until our own day were separate and local; but the lines of these great changes we have not yet clearly traced or studiously enough considered. To distinguish them and provide for them is the task which is to test the statesmanship of our generation; and it is already plain that, great as they are, these new combinations of interest have not yet gone so far as to make the States mere units of local government. Not our legal conscience merely, but our practical interests as well, call upon us to discriminate and be careful, with the care of men who handle the vital stuff of a great constitutional government.

The United States are not a single, homogeneous community. In spite of a certain superficial sameness which seems to impart to Americans a common type and point of view, they still contain communities at almost every stage of development, illustrating in their social and economic structure almost every modern variety of interest and prejudice, following occupations of every kind, in climates of every sort that the temperate zone affords. This variety of fact and condition, these substantial economic and social contrasts, do not in all cases follow state lines. They are often contrasts between region and region rather than between State and State. But they are none the less real, and are in many instances permanent and ineradicable.

From the first the United States have been socially and economically divided into regions rather than into States. The New England States have always been in most respects of a piece; the southern States have had always more interests in common than points of contrast; and the Middle States were so similarly compounded even in the day of

the erection of the government that they might without
material inconvenience have been treated as a single economic and political unit.  These first members of the Union
did, indeed, have an intense historical individuality which
made them easily distinguishable and rendered it impossible,
had any one dreamed of it, to treat them as anything but
what they were, actual communities, quick with a character
and purpose of their own.  Throughout the earlier process
of our national expansion, States formed themselves, for
the most part, upon geographical lines marked out by nature,
within the limiting flood of great rivers or the lifted masses
of great mountain chains, with here and there a mere
parallel of latitude for frontier, but generally within plots
of natural limit where those who set up homes felt some
essential and obvious tie of political union draw them together.  In later years, when States were to be created
upon the great plains which stretched their fertile breadths
upon the broad mid-surfaces of the continent, the lines
chosen for boundaries were those which had been run by
the theodolite of the public surveyor, and States began to be
disposed upon the map like squares upon a great chess-
board, where the human pieces of the future game of politics
might come to be moved very much at will and no distinct
economic, though many social, varieties were to be noted
among neighbor commonwealths.

But, while division by survey instead of by life and
historical circumstance no doubt created some artificial
political divisions, with regard to which the old theories of
separate political sovereignty seemed inapplicable enough,
the contrasts between region and region were in no way
affected; and resemblances were rendered no more striking than the differences which remained.  We have been

familiar from the first with groups of States united in interest and character; we have been familiar from the first, also, with groups of States contrasted by obvious differences of occupation and of development. These differences are almost as marked now as they ever were, and the vital growth of the nation depends upon our recognizing and providing for them. It will be checked and permanently embarrassed by ignoring them.

We are too apt to think that our American political system is distinguished by its central structure, by its President and Congress and courts, which the Constitution of the Union set up. As a matter of fact, it is distinguished by its local structure, by the extreme vitality of its parts. It would be an impossibility without its division of powers. From the first America has been a nation in the making. It has come to maturity by the stimulation of no central force or guidance, but by an abounding self-helping, self-sufficing energy in its parts, which severally brought themselves into existence and added themselves to the Union, pleasing first of all themselves in the framing of their laws and constitutions, not asking leave to exist and constitute themselves, but existing first and asking leave afterwards, self-originated, self-constituted, self-confident, self-sustaining, veritable communities, demanding only recognition. Communities develop, not by external but by internal forces. Else they do not live at all. Our commonwealths have not come into existence by invitation, like plants in a tended garden; they have sprung up of themselves, irrepressible, a sturdy, spontaneous product of the nature of men nurtured in a free air.

It is this spontaneity and variety, this independent and irrepressible life of its communities, that has given our system its extraordinary elasticity, which has preserved it from the paralysis which has sooner or later fallen upon every people who have looked to their central government to patronize and nurture them. It is this, also, which has made our political system so admirable an instrumentality of vital constitutional understandings. Throughout these lectures I have described constitutional government as that which is maintained upon the basis of an intimate understanding between those who conduct government and those who obey it. Nowhere has it been possible to maintain such understandings more successfully or with a nicer adjustment to every variety of circumstance than in the United States. The distribution of the chief powers of government among the States is the localization and specialization of constitutional understandings; and this elastic adaptation of constitutional processes to the various and changing conditions of a new country and a vast area has been the real cause of our political success.

The division of powers between the States and the federal government effected by our federal Constitution was the normal and natural division for this purpose. Under it the States possess all the ordinary legal choices that shape a people's life. Theirs is the whole of the ordinary field of law; the regulation of domestic relations and of the relations between employer and employe, the determination of property rights and of the validity and enforcement of contracts, the definition of crimes and their punishment, the definition of the many and subtle rights and obligations which lie outside the fields of property and contract, the establishment of the laws of incorporation and of the rules governing the conduct of every kind of business. The presumption insisted upon by the courts in every argument with regard to the powers of the federal government is that it has no power not explicitly granted it by the federal Constitution or reasonably to be inferred as the natural or necessary accompaniment of the powers there indisputably conveyed to it; but the presumption with regard to the powers of the States they have always held to be of exactly the opposite kind. It is that the States of course possess every power that government has ever anywhere exercised, except only those powers which their own constitutions or the Constitution of the United States explicitly or by plain inference withhold. They are the ordinary governments of the country; the federal government is its instrument only for particular purposes.

Congress is, indeed, the immediate government of the people. It does not govern the States, but acts directly upon individuals, as directly as the governments of the States themselves. It does not stand at a distance and look on, — to be ready for an occasional interference, — but is the immediate and familiar instrument of the people in everything that it undertakes, as if there were no States. The States do not stand between it and the people. It is as intimate as they in its contact with the affairs of the country's life. But the field of its action is distinct, restricted, definite.

We are not concerned in our present discussion with its powers as representative of the people in regulating the foreign affairs of the country. The discussion of the relation of the States to the federal government does not touch that field. About it there has never been doubt or debate. Neither is the power of the federal government to tax, or to regulate the military establishments of the country, any longer in dispute, even though the federal government use its power to tax to accomplish many an indirect object of economic stimulation or control which touches the independent industrial choices of the States very nearly. The one source from which all debatable federal powers of domestic regulation now spring is the power to regulate commerce between the States.

The chief object of the Union and of the revision of the Articles of Confederation which gave us our present federal Constitution was undoubtedly commercial regulation. It was not political but economic warfare between the States which threatened the existence of the new Union and made every prospect of national growth and independence doubtful, — the warfare of selfish commercial regulation. It was intended, accordingly, that the chief, one might almost say the only, domestic power of Congress in respect of the daily life of the people should be the power to regulate commerce.

It seemed a power susceptible of very simple definition at the first. Only in our own day of extraordinary variation from the older and simpler types of industry has it assumed aspects both new and without limit of variety. It is now no longer possible to frame any simple or comprehensive definition of "commerce." Above all is it difficult to distinguish the "commerce" which is confined within the boundaries of a single State and subject to its domestic regulation from that which passes from State to State and lies within the jurisdiction of Congress. The actual interchange of goods, which, strictly speaking, is commerce, within the narrow and specific meaning of the term, is now so married to their production under our great modern industrial combinations, organization and community of interest have so obscured the differences between the several parts of business which once it was easy to discriminate, that the power to regulate commerce subtly extends its borders every year into new fields of enterprise and pries into every matter of economic effort.

Added to this doubt and difficulty of analysis which makes it a constant matter of debate what the powers of Congress are is the growing dissatisfaction with the part the States are playing in the economic life of the day. They either let the pressing problems of the time alone and attempt no regulation at all, however loudly opinion and circumstance itself may call for it, or they try every half-considered remedy, embark upon a thousand experiments, and bring utter confusion upon the industry of the country by contradicting and offsetting each other's measures. No two States act alike. Manufacturers and carriers who serve commerce in many States find it impossible to obey the laws of all, and the enforcement of the laws of the States in all their variety threatens the country with a new war of conflicting regulations as serious as that which made the Philadelphia convention of 1787 necessary and gave us a new federal Constitution. This conflict of laws in matters which vitally interest the whole country, and in which no State or region can wisely stand apart to serve any peculiar interest of its own, constitutes the greatest political danger of our day. It is more apt and powerful than any other cause to bring upon us radical and ill-considered changes. It confuses our thinking upon essential matters and makes us hasty reformers out of mere impatience. We are in danger of acting before we clearly know what we want or comprehend the consequences of what we do, — in danger of altering the character of the government in order to escape a temporary inconvenience.

We are an industrial people. The development of the resources of the country, the command of the markets of the world, is for the time being more important in our eyes than any political theory or lawyer's discrimination of functions. We are intensely "practical," moreover, and insist that every obstacle, whether of law or fact, be swept out of the way. It is not the right temper for constitutional understandings. Too "practical" a purpose may give us a government such as we never should have chosen had we made the choice more thoughtfully and deliberately. We cannot afford to belie our reputation for political sagacity and self-possession by any such hasty processes as those into which such a temper of mere impatience seems likely to hurry us.

The remedy for ill-considered legislation by the States, the remedy alike for neglect and mistake on the part of their several governments, lies, not outside the States, but within them. The mistakes which they themselves correct will sink deeper into the consciousness of their people than the mistakes which Congress may rush in to correct for them, thrusting upon them what they have not learned to desire. They will either themselves learn their mistakes, by such intimate and domestic processes as will penetrate very deep and abide with them in convincing force, or else they will prove that what might have been a mistake for other States or regions of the country was no mistake for them, and the country will have been saved its wholesome variety. In no case will their failure to correct their own measures prove that the federal government might have forced wisdom upon them.

There is, however, something else that comes to the surface, and that explains not a little of our present dissatisfaction with state legislation upon matters of vital national importance. Their failure to correct their own processes may, in fact, prove that there is something radically wrong with the structure and operation of their governments, — that they have ceased to be sensitive and efficient instruments for the creation and realization of opinion, — the real function of constitutional governments.

It is better to learn the true political lesson than merely to improve business. There is something involved which is deeper than the mere question of the distribution of legislative powers within our federal system. We have come to the test of those intimate and detailed processes of self-government to which it was supposed that our principles and our experience had committed us. There are many evidences that we are losing confidence in our state legislatures, and yet it is evident that it is through them that we attempt all the more intimate measures of self-government. To lose faith in them is to lose faith in our very system of government, and that is a very serious matter. It is this loss of confidence in our local legislatures that has led our people to give so much heed to the radical suggestions of change made by those who advocate the use of the initiative and the referendum in our processes of legislation, the virtual abandonment of the representative principle, and the attempt to put into the hands of the voters themselves the power to initiate and negative laws, — in order to enable them to do for themselves what they have not been able to get satisfactorily done through the representatives they have hitherto chosen to act for them.

Such doubts and such consequent proposals of reform should make us look deeper into this question than we have hitherto looked. It may turn out, upon examination, that

what we are really dissatisfied with is not the present distribution of powers between the state and federal authorities,
but the character of our state governments.   If they were
really governments by the people, we should not be dissatisfied with them.   We are impatient of state legislatures
because they seem to us less representative of the thoughtful
opinion of the country than Congress is.   We know that
our legislatures do not think alike, but we are not sure that
our people do not think alike.   If there is a real variety of
opinion among our people in the several regions of the country, we would be poor lovers of democratic self-government
were we to wish to see those differences overridden by the
majorities of a central legislature.   It is to be hoped that
we still sufficiently understand the real processes of political
life to know that a growing country must grow, that opinion
such as government can be based upon develops by experi
ence, not by authority, that a region forced is a region dissatisfied, and that spontaneous is better, more genuine,
more permanent, than forced agreement.

The truth is that our state governments are, many of them,
no longer truly representative governments.   We are not,
in fact, dissatisfied with local representative assemblies
and the government which they impose; we are dissatisfied,
rather, with regulations imposed by commissions and
assemblies which are no longer representative.   It is a
large subject, of many debatable parts, and I can only touch
upon it here, but the fact is that we have imposed an
impossible task upon our voters, and that because it is impossible, they do not perform it.   It is impossible for the
voters of any busy community actually to pick out or in
any real sense choose the very large number of persons we
call upon them under our present state constitutions to

elect.   They have neither the time nor the quick and easy
means of coöperation which would enable them to make up
the long lists of candidates for offices, local and national,
upon which they are expected to act.   They must of
necessity leave the selection to a few persons who, from one
motive or another, volunteer to make a business of it.
These are the political bosses and managers whom the people
obey and affect to despise.   It is unjust to despise them.
Under a system of innumerable nominations they are
indispensable.   A system of so-called popular elections
like ours could not be operated successfully without them.
But it is true that by their constant and professional attention to the business of nomination a real popular choice of
candidates is done away with entirely, and that our state
officers and legislators are in effect appointed, not elected.
The question at an election is only which set of appointees
shall be put into office, those appointed by the managers
and bosses of this party or of that.   It is this, whether our
people are distinctly conscious of it or not, which has so
seriously impaired their confidence in the state legislatures
and which has made them look about for new means by
which to obtain a real choice in affairs.

Members of Congress are themselves voted for on the
lists which the local managers prepare, are themselves appointed to their candidacy as the candidates for local
functions are, but, because they are relatively few in number,
national attention is more or less concentrated upon them.
There is a more general interest in their selection, by which
party managers are sure to be somewhat checked and
guided.   After their election, moreover, they become
members of an assembly highly organized and disciplined,
and are under a very strict party responsibility in which

the personal force and character of the Speaker of the House play a greater part than their own. The man by whom they are led is scarcely less conspicuous as a national figure than the President himself, and ordinary members are but wheels in a great piece of machinery which is made sensitive to opinion in ways which local managers in no sort control. The opinion of the whole country beats upon them. The country feels, therefore, that, however selected, they are in some sense more representative, more to be depended on to register the thoughtful judgments of the country itself, than the members of state legislatures are.

It is for this reason as much as for any other that the balance of powers between the States and the federal government now trembles at an unstable equilibrium, and we hesitate into which scale to throw the weight of our purpose and preference with regard to the legislation by which we shall attempt to thread the maze of our present economic needs and perplexities. It may turn out that what our state governments need is not to be sapped of their powers and subordinated to Congress, but to be reorganized along simpler lines which will make them real organs of popular opinion. A government must have organs; it cannot act inorganically, by masses. It must have a law-making body; it can no more make law through its voters than it can make law through its newspapers.

It would be fatal to our political vitality really to strip the States of their powers and transfer them to the federal government. It cannot be too often repeated that it has been the privilege of separate development secured to the several regions of the country by the Constitution, and not the privilege of separate development only, but also that other more fundamental privilege that lies back of it, the privilege of independent local opinion and individual conviction, which has given speed, facility, vigor, and certainty to the processes of our economic and political growth. To buy temporary ease and convenience for the performance of a few great tasks of the hour at the expense of that would be to pay too great a price and to cheat all generations for the sake of one.

Undoubtedly the powers of the federal government have grown, have even grown enormously, since the creation of the government; and they have grown for the most part without amendment of the Constitution. But they have grown in almost every instance by a process which must be regarded as perfectly normal and legitimate. The Constitution cannot be regarded as a mere legal document, to be read as a will or a contract would be. It must, of the necessity of the case, be a vehicle of life. As the life of the nation changes so must the interpretation of the document which contains it change, by a nice adjustment, determined, not by the original intention of those who drew the paper, but by the exigencies and the new aspects of life itself. Changes of fact and alterations of opinion bring in their train actual extensions of community of interest, actual additions to the catalogue of things which must be included under the general terms of the law. The commerce of great systems of railway is, of course, not the commerce of wagon roads, the only land commerce known in the days when the Constitution was drafted. The common interests of a nation bound together in thought and interest and action by the telegraph and the telephone, as well as by the rushing mails which every express train carries, have a scope and variety, an infinite multiplication and intricate interlacing of which a simpler day can have had no conception.

Every general term of the Constitution has come to have a meaning as varied as the actual variety of the things which the country now shares in common.

The character of the process of constitutional adaptation depends first of all upon the wise or unwise choice of statesmen, but ultimately and chiefly upon the opinion and purpose of the courts. The chief instrumentality by which the law of the Constitution has been extended to cover the facts of national development has of course been judicial interpretation, — the decisions of the courts. The process of formal amendment of the Constitution was made so difficult by the provisions of the Constitution itself that it has seldom been feasible to use it; and the difficulty of formal amendment has undoubtedly made the courts more liberal, not to say more lax, in their interpretation than they would otherwise have been. The whole business of adaptation has been theirs, and they have undertaken it with open minds, sometimes even with boldness and a touch of audacity. But, though they have sometimes been lax, though they have sometimes yielded, it may be, to the pressure of popular agitation and of party interest, they have not often overstepped the bounds of legitimate extension. By legitimate extension I mean extension which does not change the character of the federal power, but only its items, — which does not make new kinds but only new particulars of power. Facts change and are taken care of, but principles do not change.

The members of courts are necessarily men of their own generation: we would not wish to have them men of another. Constitutional law, as well as statesmanship, must look forward, not backward, and, while we should wish the courts to be conservative, we should certainly be deeply

o

uneasy were they to hold affairs back from their natural alteration. Change as well as stability may be conservative. Conservative change is conservative, not of prejudices, but of principles, of established purposes and conceptions, the only things which in government or in any other field of action can abide. Conservative progress is a process, not of revolution, but of modification. In our own case and in the matter now under discussion it consists in a slowly progressive modification and transfer of functions as between the States and the federal government along the lines of actual development, along the lines of actual and substantial alterations of interest and of that national consciousness which is the breath of all true amendment, — and not along lines of party or individual purpose, nor by way of desperate search for remedies for existing evils.

No doubt, courts must "make" law for their own day, must have the insight which adapts law to its uses, rather than its uses to it, must sometimes venture upon decisions which have a certain touch of statesmanlike initiative in them. We shall often find ourselves looking to them for strong and fearless opinions. But there are two kinds of "strong" opinions, as a distinguished English jurist long ago pointed out. There are those which are strong with the strength of insight and intelligence and those which are strong with the mere strength of will. The latter sort all judges who act with conscience, mindful of their oaths of office, should eschew as they would eschew the actual breaking of the law. That the federal courts should have such a conscience is essential to the integrity of our whole national action. Actual alterations of interest in the make-up of our national life, actual, unmistakable changes in our national consciousness, actual modifications in our national activities such as give a new aspect and significance to the well-known purposes of our fundamental law, should, of course, be taken up into decisions which add to the number of things of which the national government must take cognizance and attempt to control. That is a function of insight and intelligence. The courage it calls for on the part of the courts is the courage of conviction. But they are, on the other hand, called on to display the more noble courage which defends ancient convictions and established principle against the clamor, the class interests, and the changeful moods of parties. They should never permit themselves wilfully to seek to find in the phrases of the Constitution remedies for evils which the federal government was never intended to deal with.

Moral and social questions originally left to the several States for settlement can be drawn into the field of federal authority only at the expense of the self-dependence and efficiency of the several communities of which our complex body politic is made up. Paternal morals, morals enforced by the judgment and choices of the central authority at Washington, do not and cannot create vital habits or methods of life unless sustained by local opinion and purpose, local prejudice and convenience, — unless supported by local convenience and interest; and only communities capable of taking care of themselves will, taken together, constitute a nation capable of vital action and control. You cannot atrophy the parts without atrophying the whole. Deliberate adding to the powers of the federal government by sheer judicial authority, because the Supreme Court can no longer be withstood or contradicted in the States, both saps the legal morality upon which a sound constitutional system must rest, and deprives the federal structure as a whole of that vitality which has given the Supreme Court itself its increase of power. It is the alchemy of decay.

It would certainly mean that we had acquired a new political temper, never hitherto characteristic of us, that we had utterly lost confidence in what we set out to do, were we now to substitute abolition for reform, — were we by degrees to do away with our boasted system of self-government out of mere impatience and disgust, like those who got rid of an instrument they no longer knew how to use.

There are some hopeful signs that we may be about to return to the better way of a time when we knew how to restrict government and adapt it to our uses in accordance with principles we did not doubt, but adhered to with an ardent fervor which was the best evidence of youth and virility. We have long been painfully conscious that we have failed in the matter of city government. It is an age of cities, and if we cannot govern our cities, we cannot govern at all. For a little while we acted as if in despair. We began to strip our city governments of their powers and to transfer them to state commissions or back to the legislatures of the States, very much as we are now stripping the States of their powers and putting them in the hands of federal commissions. The attempt was made to put the police departments of some of our cities, for example, in the hands of state officers, and to put the granting of city franchises back into the hands of the central legislature of the State, in the hope, apparently, that a uniform regulation of such things by the opinion of the whole State might take the place of corrupt control by city politicians. But it did not take us long, fortunately, to see that we were moving in the wrong direction. We have now turned to the better way of reconsidering the whole question of the organization of city governments, and are likely within a generation to purify them by simplifying them, to moralize them by placing their government in the hands of a few persons who can really be selected by popular preference instead of by the private processes of nomination by party managers, and who, because few and conspicuous, can really be watched and held to a responsibility which they will honor because they cannot escape.

It is to be hoped that we shall presently have the same light dawn upon us with regard to our state governments, and, instead of upsetting an ancient system, hallowed by long use and deep devotion, revitalize it by reorganization. And that, not only because it is an old system long beloved, but also because we are certified by all political history of the fact that centralization is not vitalization. Moralization is by life, not by statute; by the interior impulse and experience of communities, not by fostering legislation which is merely the abstraction of an experience which may belong to a nation as a whole or to many parts of it without having yet touched the thought of the rest anywhere to the quick. The object of our federal system is to bring the understandings of constitutional government home to the people of every part of the nation, to make them part of their consciousness as they go about their daily tasks. If we cannot successfully effect its adjustments by the nice local adaptations of our older practice, we have failed as constitutional statesmen.

# VIII

## PARTY GOVERNMENT IN THE UNITED STATES

In order to understand the organization and operation
of parties in the United States, it is necessary to turn once
more to the theory upon which our federal and, for that
matter, our state governments, also, were constructed.
They were, in their make-up, Whig inventions.  At the time
our national government was erected, the Whig party in
England was engaged in a very notable struggle to curb
and regulate the power of the Crown.  The struggle had
begun long before the revolution which cut our politics
asunder from the politics of England, and that revolution
itself was only an acute manifestation of the great forces
which were at work among thoughtful Englishmen everywhere.  The revolution which separated America from
England was part of a great Whig contest with the Crown
for constitutional liberties.  The leaders of that revolution
held Whig doctrine; the greater Whig statesmen on the
other side of the water recognized them as their allies and
gave them their outspoken sympathy, perceiving that they
were but fighting a battle which must sooner or later be
fought in England, whether with arms or with votes and
the more pacific strategy of politics.  Every historian now
sees that the radical changes made in the government of
England during the nineteenth century were quickened
and given assurance of success by the changes which had
preceded them in America; that the leaders of the American

198

Revolution had but taken precedence of the Whigs at home in bringing government into a new and responsible relationship to the people who were its subjects.

The theory of the Whigs in England did not go the length of seeking to destroy the power of the throne. It probably would not have gone that length in America if the throne had been on this side of the water, a domestic instead of a separate and distant power. The men in the old country to whom the American revolutionists showed the way sought only to offset the Crown with other influences, — influences of opinion acting through a reformed and purified representative chamber, whose consent not only should be necessary to the enactment of law, but the advice of whose leaders the king should find it necessary to heed; and the influences of judicial opinion acting through stable and independent courts. It was, as I have already pointed out, this theory of checks and balances, which I have called the Newtonian theory of government, that prevailed in the convention which framed the Constitution of the United States, — which prevailed over the very different theory of Hamilton, that government was not a thing which you could afford to tie up in a nice poise, as if it were to be held at an inactive equilibrium, but a thing which must every day act with straightforward and unquestionable power, with definite purpose and consistent force, choosing its policies and making good its authority, like a single organism, — the theory which would have seemed to Darwin the theory of nature itself, the nature of men as well as the nature of animal organisms. Dominated by the immediate forces and aspirations of their own day, ruled in thought and action by the great contest in which they had found themselves engaged, to hold the royal power off from arbitrary interference with their interests and their liberties, they allowed themselves to become more interested in providing checks to government than in supplying it with energy and securing to it the necessary certainty and consistency of action. They set legislature off against executive, and the courts against both, separated the three in sphere and power, and yet made the agreement of all three necessary to the operation of the government. The boast of the writers in the *Federalist* was of the perfection with which the convention at Philadelphia had interpreted Whig theory and embodied Whig dynamics in the Constitution. Mr. Hamilton's theory, that government was an affair of coöperative and harmonious forces, and that the danger of coördinate and coequal powers such as the framers of the Constitution had set up was that they might at their will pull in opposite directions and hold the government at a deadlock which no constitutional force could overcome and yet many situations might render inconvenient, if not hazardous, the temper and circumstances of the time gave public men little inclination to heed. Checks and balances were then the orthodox gospel of government.

The most serious success of the convention in applying Whig theory to the government they were constructing was the complete separation of Congress and the executive which they effected. The English Whigs fought for long to oust the Crown from the power and intimate influence it had had in the House of Commons through its control of members' seats and its corrupting power of patronage: they succeeded only in placing the leaders of the Commons itself in executive authority in the stead of the Crown. The real executive authority of the English government is vested in the ministers of the day, who are in effect a committee of the House of Commons, and legislature and executive work together under a common party organization. The one is only an agency of the other: the ministers act for their party in the House. The separation of parliament and the Crown which the reformers of the early part of the last century finally succeeded in effecting was not, in fact, a separation of the legislature from the executive, but only a separation of the real from the nominal executive. They entirely succeeded in making the king a modern "constitutional" monarch, — a monarch, that is, who, notwithstanding the dignity with which he is still surrounded and the very considerable influence which he can still exercise by reason of his station, his personal force, should he happen to have any, and his intimate access to the counsels of the executive ministry, merely "reigns" and does not govern. His choice of advisers the House of Commons dictates. But our constitution-makers did their work during the earlier part of the struggle, when it seemed merely a contest to offset the authority of the king with effectual checks, and long before it had become evident that the outcome would be the substitution of an executive which represented the popular house for one which did not. Having a free hand and a clean sheet of paper upon which to write, there was nothing to hinder the complete realization of their ideal. They succeeded in actually separating legislature and executive.

It may be that circumstances rendered their success more complete than they had intended. There is no reason to believe that they meant actually to exclude the President and his advisers from all intimate personal consultation with the houses in session. No doubt the President and the members of his cabinet could with perfect legal propriety and without any breach of the spirit of the Constitution attend the sessions of either the House or the Senate and take part in their discussions, at any rate to the extent of answering questions and explaining any measures which the President might see fit to urge in the messages which the Constitution explicitly authorizes him to send to Congress. But after a few brief attempts to institute a practice of that kind, in the early days of General Washington's administration, actual usage established another habit in respect of the intercourse between the executive and Congress, and later days have shown the houses very jealous of any attempt to establish such an intimacy. Executive officers would be most unwelcome in the houses. Their doors are shut against them. Only the door of a committee room here and there opens to receive them, and they enter only when they are invited.

In what I have said in a previous lecture of the remarkable and, in some respects, unexpected development of the President's influence and functions, I have already pointed out one of the most interesting and significant results of this absolute application of early Whig theory to the practice of our government. Its result has been that, so far as the government itself is concerned, there is but one national voice in the country, and that is the voice of the President. His isolation has quite unexpectedly been his exaltation. The House represents localities, is made up of individuals whose interest is the interest of separate and scattered constituencies, who are drawn together, indeed, under a master, the Speaker, but who are controlled by no national force except that of their party, a force outside the government rather than within it. The Senate represents in its turn regions and interests distinguished by many conflicting and contrasted purposes, united only by exterior party organization and a party spirit not generated within the chamber itself. Only the President represents the country as a whole, and the President himself is coöperatively bound to the houses only by the machinery and discipline of party, not as a person and functionary, but as a member of an outside organization which exists quite independently of the executive and legislature.

It is extraordinary the influence the early Whig theory of political dynamics has had amongst us and the far-reaching consequences which have ensued from it. It is far from being a democratic theory. It is, on the contrary, a theory whose avowed object, at any rate as applied in America, was to keep government at a sort of mechanical equipoise by means of a standing amicable contest among its several organic parts, each of which it seeks to make representative of a special interest in the nation. It is particularly intended to prevent the will of the people as a whole from having at any moment an unobstructed sweep and ascendency. And yet in every step we have taken with the intention of making our governments more democratic, we have punctiliously kept to Whig mechanics. The process shows itself most distinctly and most systematically in the structure of our state governments. We have supposed that the way to make executive offices democratic in character and motive was to separate them in authority,—to prescribe each officer's duties by statute, however petty and naturally subordinate in kind those duties might be, to put it to the voter to elect him separately, and to make him responsible, not to any superior officer set over him, but only to the courts, — thus making him a law unto himself so far as any other official is concerned.

So far have we carried the theory of checks and balances, the theory of the independence of the several organs of government.

The operation of the system is worth looking into more closely for a moment. Not very long ago a mob of unmasked men rescued a prisoner with whom they sympathized from the sheriff of a county in one of our States. The circumstances of the rescue made it very evident that the sheriff had made no serious attempt to prevent the rescue. He had had reason to expect it, and had provided no sufficient armed guard for his prisoner. The case was so flagrant that the governor of the State wrote the sheriff a sharp letter of reprimand, censuring him very justly for his neglect of duty. The sheriff replied in an open letter in which he curtly bade the governor mind his own business. The sheriff was, he said, a servant of his county, responsible to its voters and not to the governor. And his impertinence was the law itself. The governor had no more authority over him than the youngest citizen. He was responsible only to the people of his own county, from whose ranks the mob had come which had taken his prisoner away from him. He could have been brought to book only by indictment and trial, — indictment at the instance of a district attorney elected on the same "ticket" with himself, by a grand jury of men who had voted for him, and trial by a petit jury of his neighbors, whose sympathy with the rescue might be presumed from the circumstances. This is Whig dynamics in its *reductio ad particulam*. It is a species of government in solution.

It can be solidified and drawn to system only by the external authority of party, an organization outside the government and independent of it. Not being drawn together by any system provided in our constitutions, being laid apart, on the contrary, in a sort of jealous dispersion and analysis by Whig theory enacted into law, it has been necessary to keep the several parts of the government in some kind of workable combination by outside pressure, by the closely knit imperative discipline of party, a body that has no constitutional cleavages and is free to tie itself into legislative and executive functions alike by its systematic control of the *personnel* of all branches of the government. Fortunately, the federal executive is not dispersed into its many elements as the executive of each of our States is. The dispersion of our state executives runs from top to bottom. The governor has no cabinet. The executive officers of state associated with him in administration are elected as he is. Each refers his authority to particular statutes or particular clauses of the state constitution. Each is responsible politically to his constituents, the voters of the State, and, legally, to the courts and their juries. But in the federal government the executive is at least in itself a unit. Every one subordinate to the President is appointed by him and responsible to him, both legally and politically. He can control the *personnel* and the action of the whole of the great "department" of government of which he is the head. The Whig doctrine is insisted on only with regard to dealings of the legislature with the executive, and of the legislature or the executive with the courts. The three great functions of government are not to be merged or even drawn into organic coöperation, but are to be balanced against one another in a safe counterpoise. They are interdependent but organically disassociated; must coöperate, and yet are subject to no common authority.

The way in which the several branches of the federal government have been separately organized and given efficiency in the discharge of their own functions has only emphasized their separation and jealous independence. The effective organization of the House under its committees and its powerful Speaker, the organization of the Senate under its steering committees, the consolidation of the executive under the authority of the President, only render it the more feasible and the more likely that these several parts of the government will act with an all too effective consciousness of their distinct individuality and dignity, their distinct claim to be separately considered and severally obeyed in the shaping and conduct of affairs. They are not to be driven, and there is no machinery of which the Constitution knows anything by which they can be led and combined.

It is for that reason that we have had such an extraordinary development of party authority in the United States and have developed outside the government itself so elaborate and effective an organization of parties. They are absolutely necessary to hold the things thus disconnected and dispersed together and give some coherence to the action of political forces. There are, as I have already explained in another connection, so many officers to be elected that even the preparation of lists of candidates is too complicated and laborious a business to be undertaken by men busy about other things. Some one must make a profession of attending to it, must give it system and method. A few candidates for a few conspicuous offices which interested everybody, the voters themselves might select in the intervals of private business; but a multitude of candidates for offices great and small they cannot choose; and after they are chosen and elected to office they are still a multitude, and there must be somebody to look after them in the discharge of their functions, somebody to observe them closely in action, in order that they may be assessed against the time when they are to be judged. Each has his own little legal domain; there is no interdependence amongst them, no interior organization to hold them together. There must, therefore, be an exterior organization, voluntarily formed and independent of the law, whose object it shall be to bind them together in some sort of harmony and coöperation. That exterior organization is the political party. The hierarchy of its officers must supply the place of a hierarchy of legally constituted officials.

Nowhere else is the mere maintenance of the machinery of government so complex and difficult a matter as in the United States. It is not as if there were but a single government to be maintained and officered. There are the innumerable offices of States, of counties, of townships, of cities, to be filled; and it is only by elections, by the filling of offices, that parties test and maintain their hold upon public opinion. Their control of the opinion of the nation inevitably depends upon their hold on the many localities of which it is made up. If they lose their grip upon the petty choices which affect the daily life of counties and cities and States, they will inevitably lose their grip upon the greater matters, also, of which the action of the nation is made up. Parties get their coherence and prestige, their rootage and solidity, their mastery over men and events, from their command of detail, their control of the little tides that eventually flood the great channels of national action. No one realizes more completely the interdependence of municipal, state, and federal elections than do the party managers. Their parties cannot be one thing for the one set of elections and another for the other; and the complexity of the politician's task consists in the fact that, though from his point of view interdependent and intimately connected, the constantly recurring elections of a system under which everybody is elected are variously scattered in time and place and object.

We have made many efforts to separate local and national elections in time in order to separate them in spirit. Many local questions upon which the voters of particular cities or counties or States are called upon to vote have no connection whatever either in principle or in object with the national questions upon which the choice of congressmen and of presidential electors should turn. It is ideally desirable that the voter should be left free to choose the candidates of one party in local elections and the candidates of the opposite party in national elections. It is undoubtedly desirable that he should go further and separate matters of local administration from his choice of party altogether, choosing his local representatives upon their merits as men without regard to their party affiliations. We have hopefully made a score of efforts to obtain "nonpartisan" local political action. But such efforts always in the long run fail. Local parties cannot be one thing for one purpose and another for another without losing form and discipline altogether and becoming hopelessly fluid. Neither can parties form and re-form, now for this purpose and again for that, or be for one election one thing and for another another. Unless they can have local training and constant rehearsal of their parts, they will fail of coherent organization when they address themselves to the business of national elections. For national purposes they must regard themselves as parts of greater wholes, and it is impossible under such a system as our own that they should maintain their zest and interest in their business if their only objects are distant and general objects, without local rootage or illustration, centering in Congress and utterly disconnected with anything that they themselves handle. Local offices are indispensable to party discipline as rewards of local fidelity, as the visible and tangible objects of those who devote their time and energy to party organization and undertake to see to it that the full strength of the party vote is put forth when the several local sections of the party are called upon to unite for national purposes. If national politics are not to become a mere game of haphazard amidst which parties can make no calculations whatever, systematic and disciplined connections between local and national affairs are imperative, and some instrument must be found to effect them. Whatever their faults and abuses, party machines are absolutely necessary under our existing electoral arrangements, and are necessary chiefly for keeping the several segments of parties together. No party manager could piece local majorities together and make up a national majority, if local majorities were mustered upon non-partisan grounds. No party manager can keep his lieutenants to their business who has not control of local nominations. His lieutenants do not expect national rewards: their vital rootage is the rootage of local opportunity.

Just because, therefore, there is nowhere else in the world so complex and various an electoral machinery as in the United States, nowhere else in the world is party machinery so elaborate or so necessary. It is important to keep this in

P

mind.  Otherwise, when we analyze party action, we shall fall
into the too common error of thinking that we are analyzing
disease.  As a matter of fact, the whole thing is just as normal and natural as any other political development.  The
part that party has played in this country has been both
necessary and beneficial, and if bosses and secret managers
are often undesirable persons, playing their parts for their
own benefit or glorification rather than for the public good,
they are at least the natural fruits of the tree.  It has borne
fruit good and bad, sweet and bitter, wholesome and corrupt,
but it is native to our air and practice and can be uprooted
only by an entire change of system.

All the peculiarities of party government in the United
States are due to the too literal application of Whig doctrine,
to the infinite multiplication of elective offices.  There are
two things to be done for which we have supplied no ade-
quate legal or constitutional machinery: there are thousands of officials to be chosen and there are many disconnected
parts of government to be brought into coöperation.  "It
may be laid down as a political maxim that whatever
assigns to the people a power which they are naturally
incapable of wielding takes it away from them."  They
have, under our Constitution and statutes, been assigned
the power of filling innumerable elective offices; they are
incapable of wielding that power because they have neither
the time nor the necessary means of coöperative action;
the power has therefore been taken away from them, not
by law but by circumstances, and handed over to those
who have the time and the inclination to supply the necessary organization; and the system of election has been
transformed into a system of practically irresponsible
appointment to office by private party managers, — irre-

sponsible because our law has not yet been able to devise any means of making it responsible. It may also be laid down as a political maxim that when the several chief organs of government are separated by organic law and offset against each other in jealous seclusion, no common legal authority set over them, no necessary community of interest subsisting amongst them, no common origin or purpose dominating them, they must of necessity, if united at all, be united by pressure from without; and they must be united if government is to proceed. They cannot remain checked and balanced against one another; they must act, and act together. They must, therefore, of their own will or of mere necessity obey an outside master.

Both sets of dispersions, the dispersion of offices and the dispersion of functions and authorities, have coöperated to produce our parties, and their organization. Through their caucuses, their county conventions, their state conventions, their national conventions, instead of through legislatures and cabinets, they supply the indispensable means of agreement and coöperation, and direct the government of the country both in its policy and in its *personnel*. Their local managers make up the long and variegated lists of candidates made necessary under our would-be democratic practice; their caucuses and local conventions ratify the choice; their state and national conventions add declarations of principle and determine party policy. Only in the United States is party thus a distinct authority outside the formal government, expressing its purposes through its own separate and peculiar organs and permitted to dictate what Congress shall undertake and the national administration address itself to. Under every other system of government which is representative in character and which attempts to adjust the action of government to the wishes and interests of the people, the organization of parties is, in a sense, indistinguishable from the organs of the government itself. Party finds its organic lodgment in the national legislature and executive themselves. The several active parts of the government are closely united in organization for a common purpose, because they are under a common direction and themselves constitute the machinery of party control. Parties do not have to supply themselves with separate organs of their own outside the government and intended to dictate its policy, because such separate organs are unnecessary. The responsible organs of government are also the avowed organs of party. The action of opinion upon them is open and direct, not circuitous and secret.

It is interesting to observe that as a consequence the distinction we make between "politicians" and "statesmen" is peculiarly our own. In other countries where these words or their equivalents are used, the statesman differs from the politician only in capacity and in degree, and is distinguished as a public leader only in being a greater figure on the same stage, whereas with us politicians and statesmen differ in kind. A politician is a man who manages the organs of the party outside the open field of government, outside executive offices and legislative chambers, and who conveys the behests of party to those who hold the offices and make laws; while the statesman is the leader of public opinion, the immediate director (under the politicians) of executive or legislative policy, the diplomat, the recognized public servant. The politician, indeed, often holds public office and attempts the rôle of statesman as well, but, though the rôles may be combined, they are none the less sharply distinguishable. Party majorities which are actually in control of the whole legislative machinery, as party majorities in England are, determine party programs by the use of the government itself, — their leaders are at once "politicians" and "statesmen"; and, the function being public, the politician is more likely to be swallowed up in the statesman. But with us, who affect never to allow party majorities to get in complete control of governmental machinery if we can prevent it by constitutional obstacles, party programs are made up outside legislative chambers, by conventions constituted under the direction of independent politicians, — politicians, I mean, who are, at any rate in respect of that function, independent of the responsibilities of office and of public action; and these independent conventions, not charged with the responsibility of carrying out their programs, actually outline the policy of administrations and dictate the action of Congress, the irresponsible dictating to the responsible, and so, it may be, destroying the very responsibility itself. "The peculiarities of American party government are all due to this separation of party management from direct and immediate responsibility for the administration of the government."

The satisfactions of power must be very great to attract so many men of unusual gifts to attempt the hazardous and little honored business of party management. We have made it necessary that we should have "bosses" and that they and their lieutenants should assign offices by appointment, but it is a very difficult and precarious business which they undertake. It is difficult and hazardous not only because it is irregular and only partially protected by law, but also because the people look askance at it and often with a sudden disgust turn upon it and break it up, for a little while rendering it impossible. The reason for these occasional outbursts of discontent and resentment is evident and substantial enough. They come when the people happen to realize that under existing party machinery they have virtually no control at all over nominations for office, and that, having no real control over the choice of candidates, they are cut off from exercising real representative self-government, — that they have been solemnly taking part in a farce. But their revolt is only fitful and upon occasion. Reform associations arise, committees of fifty or seventy or a hundred are formed to set matters right and put government back into the hands of the people, but it is always found that no one can successfully supplant the carefully devised machinery of professional politicians without taking the same pains that they take, without devoting to the business the time and the enthusiasm for details which they devote to it, or supplant the politicians themselves without forming rival organizations as competent as theirs to keep an eye on the whole complicated process of elections and platforms, without, in short, themselves becoming in their turn professional politicians. It is an odd operation of the Whig system that it should make such party organizations at once necessary and disreputable, and I should say that in view of the legal arrangements which we have deliberately made, the disrepute in which professional politicians are held, is in spirit highly unconstitutional.

There can be and there need be no national boss like the local bosses of States and cities, because federal patronage is not distributed by election. Local bosses commonly control the selection of members of Congress because the congressional districts are local, and members of Congress are voted for by local ticket; but they cannot control federal appointments without the consent of the President. By the same token, the President can, if he chooses, become national boss by the use of his enormous patronage, doling out his local gifts of place to local party managers in return for support and coöperation in the guidance and control of his party. His patronage touches every community in the United States. He can often by its use disconcert and even master the local managers of his own party by combining the arts of the politician with the duties of the statesman, and he can go far towards establishing a complete personal domination. He can even break party lines asunder and draw together combinations of his own devising. It is against this that our national civil service laws have been wisely directed.

But what really restrains him is his conspicuous position and the fact that opinion will hold him responsible for his use of his patronage. Local bosses are often very obscure persons. To the vast majority of the voters they are entirely unknown, and it is their desire to be as little in evidence as possible. They are often not themselves office-holders at all, and there is no way in which by mere elective processes they can be held responsible. But the President's appointments are public, and he alone by constitutional assignment is responsible for them. Such open responsibility sobers and restrains even where principle is lacking. Many a man who does not scruple to make in private political arrangements which will serve his own purposes will be very careful to be judicious in every act for which he is known to be singly responsible. Responsible appointments are always better than irresponsible. Responsible appointments are appointments made under scrutiny; irresponsible appointments are those made by private persons in private.

The machinery of party rule is nominally representative. The several assemblies and conventions through which the parties operate are supposed to be made up of delegates chosen by the voters of the party, to speak for them with a certain knowledge of what they want and expect. But here again the action of the voters themselves is hardly more than nominal. The lists of delegates are made up by the party managers as freely in all ordinary circumstances as are the lists of the candidates in whose selection they concur. To add the duty of really selecting delegates to the duty of selecting men for office already laid upon our voters by law would be only to add to the impossibility of their task, and to their confusion if they attempted to perform it. When difficulties arise in the process, rival bodies of delegates can always be chosen, and then the managing committees who are in charge of the party's affairs — the county committee, the state committee, or the national committee — can dictate which of the contesting delegations shall be admitted, which shall have their credentials accepted. It is to this necessity we have been brought by farming the functions of government out to outside parties. We have made the task of the voter hopeless and therefore impossible.

And yet at the best the control which party exercises over government is uncertain. There can be, whether for the voter or for the managing politician himself, little more than a presumption that what party managers propose and promise will be done, for the separation of authority between the several organs of government itself still stands in the way. Government is still in solution, and nothing may come to crystallization. But we may congratulate ourselves that we have succeeded as well as we have in giving our politics unity and coherence. We should have drifted sadly, should much oftener have been made to guess what the course of our politics should be, had we not constructed this singular and, on the whole, efficient machinery by which we have in all ordinary seasons contrived to hold the *personnel* and the policy of our government together.

Moreover, there is another use which parties thus thoroughly organized and universally active have served among us which has been of supreme importance. It is clear that without them it would hardly have been possible for the voters of the country to be united in truly national judgments upon national questions. For a hundred years or more we have been a nation in the making, and it would be hard to exaggerate the importance of the nationalizing influence of our great political parties. Without them, in a country so various as ours, with communities at every stage of development, separated into parts by the sharpest economic contrasts and social differences, with local problems and conditions of their own which seemed to give them a separate interest very difficult to combine with any other, full of keen rivalries and here and there cut athwart by deep-rooted prejudices, national opinions, national judgments, could never have been formulated or enforced without the instrumentality of well-disciplined parties which extended their organization in a close network over the whole country, and which had always their desire for office and for the power which office brings to urge as their conclusive reason,—a reason which every voter could understand, —why there should be agreement in opinion and in program as between section and section, whatever the temptation to divide and act separately, as their conclusive argument against local interest and preference. If local and national politics had ever been for long successfully divorced, this would have been impossible.

Students of our politics have not always sufficiently recognized the extraordinary part political parties have played in making a national life which might otherwise have been loose and diverse almost to the point of being inorganic a thing of definite coherence and common purpose. There is a sense in which our parties may be said to have been our real body politic. Not the authority of Congress, not the leadership of the President, but the discipline and zest of parties, has held us together, has made it possible for us to form and to carry out national programs. It is not merely that the utmost economic diversity has marked the development of the different parts of the country, and that their consciousness of different and even rival and conflicting interests has rendered the sympathy between them imperfect, the likelihood of antagonism very great indeed. There have been social differences, also, quite as marked. These social differences were no doubt themselves founded in economic diversity, but they cut much deeper than mere economic diversity of itself could have cut and made real sympathy unnatural, spontaneous coöperation between the portions of the country which they had offset against one another extremely difficult, and, in the absence of party discipline, extremely unlikely. The social contrast between the North and South before the Civil War will occur to every one, — a contrast created, of course, by the existence of the slave system in the South and deepened and elaborated by many another influence, until the political partnership of the two regions became at last actually impossible.

And yet there was no exclusive southern party, no exclusive northern party, until the war itself came.  Until then each national party had a strong and loyal following both North and South, and seemed to be conscious of no sectional lines which need prevent cordial coöperation.  The very interest which a section with peculiar needs and objects of its own had in maintaining its proportional influence in the direction of the policy of the general government, in order both to protect itself and to further such measures conceived in its own interest as it could induce the partners to concede, made it eager to escape actual political isolation and keep its representation in national party counsels.

And, though the contrast between the South with slavery and the other portions of the country without it was the sharpest and most dangerous contrast that our history has disclosed, many another crisis in our affairs has been accentuated by differences of interest and of point of view almost as great.  The feeling of the communities beyond the Alleghanies towards the communities by the Atlantic seaboard throughout all the time when foreign powers owned the southern outlet of the great valley of the Mississippi;  the feeling of the communities of the plains towards the communities to the eastward which seemed to grudge them their development and to prefer the interest of the manufacturer to the interest of the farmer;  the feeling of the mining camps towards the regions of commerce and of all the old order which got their wealth but did not understand or regard their wishes in matters of local regulation and self-government;  the circumstances in which Territories were set up and the heats in which States were forged, — these have been the difficulties and hazards of our national history, and it has been nothing less than a marvel how the network of parties has taken up and broken the restless strain of contest and jealousy, like an invisible network of kindly oil upon the disordered waters of the sea.

It is in this vital sense that our national parties have been our veritable body politic. The very compulsion of selfishness has made them serviceable; the very play of self-interest has made them effective. In organization was their strength. It brought them the rewards of local office, the command of patronage of many kinds, the detailed control of opinion, the subtle mastery of every force of growth and expansion. They strove for nothing so constantly or so watchfully as for the compact, coöperative organization and action which served to hold the nation in their hands.

But we have come within sight of the end of the merely nationalizing process. Contrasts between region and region become every year less obvious, conflicts of interest less acute and disturbing. Party organization is no longer needed for the mere rudimentary task of holding the machinery together or giving it the sustenance of some common object, some single coöperative motive. The time is at hand when we can with safety examine the network of party in its detail and change its structure without imperilling its strength. This thing that has served us so well might now master us if we left it irresponsible. We must see to it that it is made responsible.

I have already explained in what sense and for what very sufficient reasons it is irresponsible. Party organizations appoint our elective officers, and we do not elect them. The chief obstacle to their reform, the chief thing that has stood in the way of making them amenable to opinion, controllable by independent opposition, is the reverence with which we have come to regard them. By binding us together at moments of crisis they have won our affectionate fealty.  Because the Republican party "saved the Union," a whole generation went by, in many parts of the country, before men who had acted with it in a time of crisis could believe it possible for any "gentleman" or patriot to break away from it or oppose it, whatever its policy and however remote from anything it had originally professed or undertaken.  Because the Democratic party had stood for state rights and a power freely dispersed among the people, because it had tried to avoid war and preserve the old harmony of the sections, men of the same fervor of sympathy in other parts of the country deemed it equally incredible that any man of breeding or of principle could turn his back upon it or act with any other political organization.  The feeling lasted until lines of party division became equally fixed and artificial.  But with changing generations feelings change.  We are coming now to look upon our parties once more as instruments for progressive action, as means for handling the affairs of a new age. Sentimental reminiscence is less dominant over us.  We are ready to study new uses for our parties and to adapt them to new standards and principles.

The principle of change, if change there is to be, should spring out of this question: Have we had enough of the literal translation of Whig theory into practice, into constitutions?  Are we ready to make our legislatures and our executives our real bodies politic, instead of our parties?  If we are, we must think less of checks and balances and more of coördinated power, less of separation of functions and more of the synthesis of action.  If we are, we must decrease the number and complexity of the things the voter is called upon to do;  concentrate his attention upon a few men whom he can make responsible, a few objects upon which he can easily centre his purpose; make parties his instruments and not his masters by an utter simplification of the things he is expected to look to.

Every test of principle or of program returns to our original conception of constitutional government. Every study of party must turn about our purpose to have real representative institutions. Constitutional government can be vital only when it is refreshed at every turn of affairs by a new and cordial and easily attained understanding between those who govern and those who are governed. It can be maintained only by genuine common counsel; and genuine common counsel can be obtained only by genuine representative institutions. A people who know their minds and can get real representatives to express them are a self-governed people, the practised masters of constitutional government.

# INDEX

223

Q